Praise for **Sex, God,**

Sex, God, and the Single Life IS NOT your typical book on sex. Hafeez writes beautifully like a poet and powerfully like a prophet! The life-giving content in these pages will grip your heart and transform how you view sex. I highly recommend you and some of your friends buy this book and read it together.

Derwin L. Gray
Lead Pastor at Transformation Church
and Author of *Limitless Life: You Are More Than Past When God Holds Your Future*

In a transparent and thought-provoking manner, *Sex, God, and the Single Life* boldly explores an often avoided, but crucial, area of life and relationships: single sexuality. Singles are challenged to rethink cultural distortions in their sexuality and sexual relating as they learn to experience sexual intimacy and wholeness. Hafeez has written a book from his heart to ours and created an important read for both single and married Christian adults.

Dr. Doug Rosenau
Professor at the Institute for Sexual Wholeness
and Author of *A Celebration of Sex*

If you want an honest book about sexuality and you sense that God might be the key to experiencing the fullness of that, then you should read this book. Hafeez has wrestled with the tough questions, and he's found a path of freedom that others can follow.

Paula Rinehart
Author of *Sex and the Soul of a Woman*

This is an excellent book in teaching what sexuality is for and what healthy sex really is. If you are single and want to know the truth about sex and how not to pervert it, this will be a great book for you.

Stephen Arterburn
Founder and Chairman of New Life Ministries,
Host of Christian radio talk show *New Life Live!* and
Best-selling Author of the *Every Man Series*

In this amazing book, Hafeez speaks directly to the longing for intimacy that I've seen in every one of the single or single again men and women I have surveyed in my research. He shows that God's way really is the only way that will lead us to thrive, both now and in the future. Thank you, Hafeez, for sharing this truth and pointing the way for every single to experience wholeness now and in their future marriages!

Shaunti Feldhahn
Social researcher, speaker
and Author of *For Women Only* and
The Surprising Secrets of Highly Happy Marriages

Hafeez Baoku has a real passion to honor, enjoy and prioritize marriage. We need more voices like his challenging the church and couples to esteem as highly valuable the exclusivity of sexual intimacy in marriage.

Ted Cunningham
Pastor of Woodland Hills Family Church and
Author of *Fun Loving You and Trophy Child*

Hafeez has given singles a clear and provocative gift to point the way to healthy sexuality. His gift of being relevant and relational is apparent throughout the book. It is a joyful and holy read!

Dr. Ted Roberts
Founder of Pure Desire Ministries International, pastor,
Author and sexual addiction counselor

In a culture with many misconceptions about God, sex and the confusion of how they are interwoven together as a tool to bring us pleasure and Him Glory, there needs to be a voice from the young to the young that is relevant with a biblical worldview. With precision and care, Hafeez gives hope, clarity and truth to help sanitize the dysfunctional beliefs about sex in our culture.

Aaron K. Anderson
Lead Pastor at Vintage Church,
Durham, North Carolina

SEX, GOD, AND THE SINGLE LIFE

An Honest Journey to Satisfying Intimacy

HAFEEZ BAOKU

PUBLICATIONS

Fort Washington, PA 19034

Sex, God, and the Single Life

© 2014 by Hafeez Baoku
All rights reserved. Published 2014

Published by CLC Publications

U.S.A.
P.O. Box 1449, Fort Washington, PA 19034

UNITED KINGDOM
CLC International (UK)
51 The Dean, Alresford, Hampshire, SO24 9BJ

ISBN (paperback): 978-1-61958-166-1
ISBN (e-book): 978-1-61958-167-8

Printed in the United States of America

Contents

Special Thanks

I want to give a special thanks to everyone who has helped me successfully finish my first book. Thank you so much, Bill and Kitty, for telling me the truth about the blandness of my first manuscript, which motivated me to rewrite it. Thank you so much, Leigh, my first graceful editor who blessed me with the edits to my proposal and manuscript. Thank you so much to Dr. Doug, Corey, Ann and all the people at Building Intimate Marriages for providing me such wisdom and insight on the topic of sexuality from a biblical perspective. Thank you so much, Roslyn, for telling me the truth about my second manuscript, which helped me to make necessary changes. Thank you so much, Valentin, Antoine and Alberta—your generosity means the world to me. Thank you so much to the grace-filled people at CLC Publications for making my dreams and prayers come true.

Last but not least, thank You so much to my Lord and Savior Jesus Christ. Thank You so much for saving my life in college. Thank You so much for transforming my views on sexuality and giving me the wisdom and grace to talk about this issue. I love You, Lord, and I will be indebted to You forever.

Note to the Reader

Having clear language is extremely important in any conversation, especially in a conversation about sex. I know that I have to be clear with my definition of sex from the beginning in order to reduce the ambiguity around the word. When I use the word "sex" in this book, know that my definition is not limited to the act of intercourse alone but to any form of sexual behavior or relating.

Introduction

Everyone thinks about sex in either a positive way or a negative way.

If you're someone who thinks about sex in a positive way, you may be a bachelor or a bachelorette who hopes this book will provide you with ten steps to having the best sex of your life. You may be the virgin guy who is obsessed with sexual performance and doesn't want to make any sexual blunders. You may be the young girl who wants to experience the same passionate, romantic sexual situations that are portrayed in Hollywood movies such as *Titanic* or *The Notebook*. Or maybe you just love talking about sex, and you picked up this book because you want to learn everything about the topic.

I can't guarantee that this book will answer all your questions about sex and sexuality, because I don't claim to be an expert on this topic. However, I do promise to provide you with the secret to experiencing the long-lasting sexual joy and satisfaction you're searching for.

On the other hand, some of you who picked up this book may think about sex in a negative way. You may be the virgin who is harassed by your peers because you've never had sex, and you're afraid of one day becoming the dreaded forty-year-old virgin. You may be in a dating relationship and have seen how sex, or the lack of it, has destroyed the relationships of others, and you don't want the same problem to occur in your relationship. You may have grown up in church and now feel like damaged goods because of all your broken purity promises, and you struggle every day with forgiving yourself. Or, if you are similar to me, you may be single and wanting a clear understanding of sex, and you're willing to listen to anyone who will give you the answers you are looking for. If you can relate to any of these situations, then you've picked up the right book.

Pleasure-Filled Nights but Empty Mornings Full of Regret

You probably can recount many stories from friends regarding sexual decisions that they've regretted making. Or, if you are completely honest, you can likely recount stories about sexual decisions of your own that you've regretted making. I know that I can recount dozens of both of these kinds of stories.

Out of all the stories I can recall, there is one that I believe most people can relate to. One day I was having a conversation with one of my coworkers, Sarah, and we were interrupted by a phone call she received from her friend Keisha. As soon as Sarah picked up the phone, I could hear Keisha crying on the other line, screaming hysterically as if someone close to her had recently passed away. After calming down, Keisha began to tell Sarah about a guy she was interested in who had invited her to his apartment at one in the morning to watch a movie. She'd arrived at his house, and they had hooked up less than ten minutes into the movie. Keisha was crying because the guy hadn't talked to her or answered her calls since that night. She could not believe that she had allowed herself to be used by another guy—again. She hated the emptiness that came after meaningless casual sex and was ready to give up on love and any hope of finding someone who would truly care for her.

Maybe some of you can't relate to the story completely, but does the ending sound vaguely familiar? It does to me, because it's the theme of my sexual history, which is filled with decisions that I believed in the moment were good for me but in the long run always provided more pain than pleasure. Eventually, after experiencing enough hurt, I would throw in the towel and say, "I can't believe I did that again. I am so stupid. I'm done with [fill in the sexual decision here]. I am never going to do it again." But a couple months, weeks, days or hours would go by, and I'd ended up folding and making the same bad decision all over again.

How about you? Do you feel the same way I do? Are you tired of random hookups that feel good in the now but leave you feeling dry and hollow the morning afterward? Are you fed up with spending hours watching pornography that never satisfies the desires of your heart and always keeps you longing for more pleasure? Are you confused about your sexuality but too afraid to talk to someone about your struggles because you are too afraid of becoming a social outcast? Are you sick of going from one relationship to another and giving your heart, mind, body and soul to someone who "loves" you but then ends the relationship and breaks your heart as soon as things become difficult?

I grew tired of the endless cycles of bad sexual decisions that left me empty and unsatisfied in my pursuit of happiness. So I stopped looking for love in all the wrong places and living for temporary highs and decided to look for the truth about sex, which led me to writing this book. In it I want to pass on to you what I learned (oftentimes the hard way) about experiencing true sexual joy and satisfaction.

This Book Is for You

Now before we get started, I hope you have an open mind. I am not saying that this book will be the answer to all your problems about sex and sexuality, but the solutions in it have helped and transformed my life, the lives of my friends and the lives of many others I have encountered through my journey. This healing journey began when I realized that God had a lot to teach me about sex. And wait—before you put this book down because I brought God into the equation, hear me out.

When I talk about God, I'm not talking about the God of overbearing and institutionalized religion—a mean, distant stepfather who bosses people around and forces them to obey His burdensome commands. Nor am I talking about a God who is an oppressive dictator with eyes full of hate who is only concerned with rules and regulations and doesn't care about anyone's well-being or joy. When I talk about God, I am talking about a loving Father who deeply cares for all His children; a loving Father whose affection for His children isn't based on their behavior but on His own goodness; a loving Father who desires all His children to experience true joy and satisfaction in every avenue of their lives. This amazing, loving, compassionate Father is the God whom I plan to talk about in this book.

I know some of you may think what I used to believe: that God doesn't have anything enlightening or progressive to say about sex. But think about it. If God was the one who designed the human anatomy, couldn't there be a lesson or two that He can teach us about sex?

So don't worry, I'm not going to beat you over the head with the Bible. And if you're thinking that I'm writing one of those books that tell you how messed up you are, know that this is not the case. I was, and still am to a degree, in your same shoes. In my life I've made many (many) bad sexual decisions that I regret every single day, but God has opened my eyes and transformed my life so that I can move past the errors of my past and experience true sexual joy and satisfaction. This phenomenal experience that has sexually revolutionized my life is what I want to convey to you through the pages of this book.

Your journey for experiencing true sexual joy and satisfaction can only begin if you are willing to take a leap of faith and trust God's methods, which you will find in the pages of this book. And if you start this book, I hope that you will promise to finish it! As you read, you may come across certain topics that you will not agree with, but hang in there, and I promise that things will be clear by the end of the book.

So if you are ready to take this journey with me in order to find the secrets to experiencing true sexual joy and satisfaction, turn the page, and let's begin.

Part I

What Have We Already Learned about Sex?

1

Let's Talk about Sex

This chapter and the first half of the book will not make sense if you haven't read the introduction. So if you skipped the introduction, please go back and read it

"Sex" is a simple three-letter word, but the word itself is not simply understood—despite being one of the most talked-about topics in our culture. From music, movies and television to politics and the Internet, it seems as if everybody is either talking or thinking about sex.

In the 2011 *Psychology Today* article "How Often Do Men and Women Think about Sex?" it was reported that the average college-aged man thought about sex as much as he thought about food and sleep.[1] It was also reported that the average college-aged woman thought about sex from one to one hundred forty times each day. While I am not sure if I am guilty of thinking about sex as much as I think about food or sleep, I know that I've been thinking about the topic for quite a while.

My first conversation about sex occurred on the playground at elementary school with my best friend Tommy when we were in third grade. Tommy told me a story about a man who'd had sex with his cat, and afterward the cat had given birth to man-kittens (I know that the idea of a man and a cat making man-kittens sounds crazy, but when you are seven years old, you believe everything). After hearing the story, I was astonished that Tommy had such profound sexual insight at the tender age of seven. From that day on I was intrigued with the topic of sex; I had to learn everything there was to know about it.

Years later, when I entered seventh grade, I thought my dream of learning more about sex was finally about to come true. Our class had been given permission to take sexual education, or sex ed—the famous one-week sex talk in health class and the only time of year when we could say "penis" and "vagina" in school without getting in trouble.

In order to participate in sex ed, the teacher required everyone in the class to get a consent form signed by his or her parents. I thought to myself that this wouldn't be a problem. My parents would be eager to give me permission to take sex ed; there was no way they would say no. But I was wrong. Instead of checking the box that said, "Yes, I allow my child to take this class," my parents checked the box that said, "No, I don't want my child taking this class." When my parents handed the form back to me, I was heartbroken.

I can still remember how embarrassing it was being in health class when my teacher said, "Class, let's talk about sex," and then signaled for me to exit the room because I did not have permission to take the class. So during health class, as my classmates were becoming enlightened about sex, I was forced to go to the library and waste away in my sorrow and sexual ignorance.

I was not only harassed by my classmates for not being able to take sex ed, but, of all people, I was also made fun of by my homeroom teacher. She once referred to me as "Hafeez, the ghoul who haunts the halls because his mommy won't allow him to take sex ed." Fortunately for me, seventh grade flew by quickly. My classmates eventually stopped making fun of me, and I was able to put the embarrassing sex-ed ordeal behind me.

I felt sure that eighth grade would be the year I would learn everything there was to know about sex, but I was let down once again. Eighth-grade health class did not offer sex ed, because all the students were supposed to have taken it the previous year. Sadly, I was forced to wait once again for another year to go by without fully understanding sex.

Thankfully, my high school offered sex ed to incoming freshmen. I remember the day when my teacher passed out the waiver form, and I knew that this was the year I was going to learn everything there was to know about sex. This time when I brought the waiver form home, my parents checked the box that said, "Yes, my child can take this class."

I can still remember how excited I was when the first day of sex ed came around. I sat eagerly in my seat waiting to become a sexologist like all my friends were. However, the moment the teacher opened her mouth and started talking about sex, the only feeling I can remember having is disappointment.

After a whole week of sex ed, the only two sex-related topics that we'd talked about were condoms and genital herpes. The line "Use a condom, and if you don't, you're going to catch genital herpes" summed up my high-school experience with sexual education. Sex ed was nothing like I expected. I had thought the class would be filled with discussions about sexual secrets that only the teacher and special sex-help gurus knew. But it hadn't been, and I was still in the dark about the topic of sex.

After being let down once again by the education system, I started to think carefully about where I could turn next in order to gain profound insight about sex. After careful consideration I decided to go where every teenager goes in order to find any valuable information about life: their teenage friends.

Most of what I learned about sex in high school came from stories that my friends told me about their sexual escapades. Yet even with my limited understanding of sex, I realized that many of these stories were not true and did not make any sense. Unfortunately, teenagers (especially teenage boys) have a terrible habit of overexaggerating their sexual experiences and sexual knowledge. All the information I got from them ended up being useless.

After being let down by my friends, I was back to the starting point on my journey to sexual enlightenment. I still needed knowledge about sex, but I knew my immature friends couldn't offer it to me. So I decided to seek out knowledge from the next greatest teenage fountain of wisdom: Hollywood movies.

From the moment I found out that there was information about sex and sexual situations in PG-13 and R-rated movies, Hollywood became my sexual instructor and I its humble student.

After being sexually enlightened by Hollywood, I took my newfound sexual knowledge to Internet discussion boards under the pen name LoveDoctor2.0, where I counseled other sexually confused teenagers about their sexual problems. For years I thought I was an official sex expert—until I started to apply the advice I had been giving others to my own life. Then I realized that all the information Hollywood had taught me about sex was a lie as well.

Sex 101

So what about you? What is your story, and how did you learn about sex?

You probably didn't learn about sex from health class, because more than likely you fell asleep during all the uncomfortable lectures about women's menstrual cycles; you probably didn't learn about sex from your parents, because if they gave you the dreaded "birds and the bees" speech, it probably sounded like an encrypted German WWII message since they were so nervous. And you probably weren't paying attention to your church's youth-group teachings about sex because words like "abstinence," "chastity" and "celibacy" all sound like viral diseases that nobody wants to catch.

So what you learned about sex more than likely came from something or someone in culture—whether it was the Internet, movies, television, music, magazines, romance novels or your friends. But if you take a look at all the sources I've listed, you'll notice that they are not the most reliable. Let me show you what I am talking about by giving examples of what each of these "infallible" sources has to say about sex.

Learning about sex from friends. Have you ever watched a news reporter interview a local resident who was supposedly an eyewitness to a crime, and as soon as that person opened his or her mouth to talk about the incident, the individual had no idea what he or she was talking about? More than likely, this "eyewitness" was nowhere near the crime when it happened; the person only acted as if he or she had seen the crime in order to get on prime-time TV.

Listening to people who give phony news reports reminds me of what it's like to learn about sex from teenagers. As I said earlier, teenagers overexaggerate their sexual experiences and knowledge in order to prove to others that they are experts about sex. But while their bodies are physically capable of having sex, their minds are not mature enough to comprehend the true meaning of sex.

Learning about sex from the Internet. One day when I was researching the topic of sex online, I read that the average man thinks about sex every seven seconds.[2] At first I believed this, but when I did the math, I realized that this was impossible. If this claim was true, it meant that the average man thinks about sex 12,343 times a day. I'm not sure that even sex addicts think about sex that much. If all our sexual knowledge comes from the Internet, we're in for some trouble. The *Huffington Post* reported that more than 90 percent of people distrust the information they find on the Internet.[3] Why? Because they believe that it is faulty information.

Learning about sex from music. Have you noticed that most R&B artists will release an amazing single about sex and the pleasure they receive from it but on their next single be upset because of the heartbreak they experienced from a broken relationship? How do these artists always end up so miserable? If you don't believe me, make a list of your favorite R&B songs or other slow songs and look at the life of the artist who sang or wrote them. You'll see that I am not making this up.

It's hard to trust what musicians teach about sex, because these people seem to be more sexually empty and confused than we are.

Learning about sex from romance novels. One day during English class I took a look into one of my friend's Zane novels—an African-American sex novel that mainly caters to young women. After reading a couple pages, I didn't know which was more real—the story of the sexual experiences in the book or the story of the Easter bunny. Every single character in the book was having passionate sex and was perfectly sexually satisfied every time, and every one of them was having an affair with his or her neighbor without getting caught.

After reading those books I realized that there wasn't a single sexual situation that occurs in these romance novels that happens in real life. It turns out that romance novels are in the fiction section of the bookstore for a reason.

Learning about sex from magazines. Virtually every magazine today has some type of article related to sex. Even magazines that have nothing to do with sex—such as those about cooking, cars or gardening—have articles that are sex related. "Ten Steps to Having the Best Sex Now" is what these magazines promise to teach their readers.

Unfortunately, these magazines also give terrible sexual advice, because their advice is written by foolish, desperate people to other foolish, desperate people. I believe the reason that these magazines make so much money is that people always buy the next issue since the advice they received in the previous issue didn't solve their sexual problems.

Learning about sex from Hollywood. When it comes to learning about sex from television and Hollywood movies, everyone knows that the sexual situations and story lines in them are completely fictional. Have you ever wondered why the characters in every Hollywood movie always have casual, unprotected sex in random places but never seem to get pregnant? Or how the characters in the movies have sex for long hours, but afterward their hair and makeup remain perfectly intact? Am I the only person not seeing something add up? It's hard to learn about sex from Hollywood, because the sexual situations it portrays don't happen in real life.

Can Someone Please Help Us?

If we are going to learn the secrets of experiencing true joy and sexual satisfaction, I don't believe that our misinformed culture can provide us with the wisdom we need. Everyone around us is as sexually confused as we are.

Tim Alan Gardner put it best:

> We are more sexually informed than ever. We can take advantage of therapy and medical treatments not available to previous generations. And we have free access to more sexually stimulating material than at any time in history. But despite all this knowledge, people are more sexually empty, more sexually frustrated and more sexually lost than ever before.[4]

Are you starting to feel as if you've been cheated in regard to your sexual education? I know I felt that way. After being let down by source after source, I thought that I was doomed to spend the rest of my life in sexual ignorance.

So what happens next after we come to this conclusion? Who will we turn to when everything else in life fails to teach us the truth about sex? The answer is easy. We do what I did, which is to resort to learning about sex from the only possible source that we believe will never let us down: me, myself and I.

Reflection

- When you hear the word "sex," what is the first thought that comes to your mind?
- Where did you originally learn about sex?
- Who or what in culture has primarily educated you about sex?

2

Whom Do You Trust for Advice about Sex?

After being let down by the misconceptions about sex that I gained from culture and others, I became somewhat of a hermit and tried to find the truth in isolation. I developed my own purpose and definition for sex by giving it a face (whom I had sex with: boy, girl or both) and a place (the context I had sex in: marriage, with a committed partner or with a random person). My definition was based on my feelings, my experiences and what I believed was right. I was pretty sure that the idea of sex being only for marriage was as old school an idea as an 8-track, so I went with a more modern definition: I should be free to have sex with whatever girl I desired. This led to a period of sexual experimentation in my life as I sought to achieve the fulfillment I longed for.

Since having relationships with the girls at my school had always ended in disappointment for me, to satisfy my needs I turned to the problem-free cyber girls in Internet pornography. Because I was so desperately looking for someone or something to fulfill me, I believed that pornography would be the solution to all my sexual desires. I thought it would be good for me, since it made me feel good, but I was wrong. The more I viewed pornography, the more difficult it was for me to connect to reality—especially to real women. I constantly compared and contrasted the women I saw in person to the women I viewed on the Internet. Because of my false expectations, I could not find a girl who met the impossible sexual standard that me and my perfectly photoshopped cyber models had set for her.

Even though I attempted to stop watching pornography on multiple occasions, I couldn't—I was addicted, and pornography was controlling my life. Regardless of the pleasure I received from Internet pornography, it seemed to never satisfy my sexual needs. It was as if I was dying of thirst in the middle of the Sahara, and porn was a canteen of salt water. Time and time again I drank of it, and it met my temporal needs, yet it was always only a matter of time, and I wanted more and more and more.

The very sexual definition that I had created and believed would bring me fulfillment and happiness was ruining my life and any possibility of experiencing the joy and satisfaction that I wanted. It was as if I was using a knife to stop my heart from bleeding—my actions only added more pain to my problem.

Am I the Only One Feeling This Way?

I believe that many of you can relate to my story.

After listening to everything that culture and your friends taught you about sex, you began to engage in sexual actions that you believed would satisfy you. After going from one empty encounter to another, you always woke up the next morning as lonely and empty as you had been before, even if you sometimes experienced nights of ecstasy.

You may be the guy who has bought into the idea that experiencing sexual pleasure from multiple women (real or virtual) will satisfy all your physical and emotional desires and make you a man. So you go from woman to woman, living your life in the pursuit of self-gratification. At times you have fun due to the pleasure you're receiving, but you're not satisfied. When you wake up in the morning, you aren't happy. There is still an itch deep down inside you that isn't being scratched. It seems as though there is something more than temporary pleasure that you long to be satisfied with, but you don't know what it could be.

Or maybe you're the girl who desperately wants to be loved, so you give your heart and body to any guy who is willing to show you attention. At times you're happy, because a guy is showing you the affection and attention that you desire, but you still aren't satisfied, because you know that he is only using you as a means to satisfy himself. You desperately want to experience true love and intimacy, but your on-again, off-again boyfriend (or friend with benefits) doesn't seem able to give it to you. The tears of loneliness that you cry when you are alone at night show that something is missing in your life, but you don't know what it could be.

If you can relate to either of those scenarios, don't worry—you are not alone. After talking with hundreds of people about this issue, I've found that most people to some degree feel this way, but everyone is too nervous to say that they are hurting. We don't want people to look at us and ask, "What's wrong with you? How can sex be so hurtful when it's so much fun? You must not be doing it right."

Interestingly enough, many studies show that most people are not getting sex right.

One of the leading causes for divorce or breakup each year is due to sex-related issues.[1] Studies among sexually active college students show that 44 percent of people say that someone has been hurt emotionally due to their sexual behavior[2] (personally, I believe that the person who got hurt was more than likely themselves). By the age of twenty-four, one in three sexually active people will have contracted a sexually transmitted infection.[3] These results show us that millions of people have problems with sex and sexuality, whether they are single or married.

This issue with sex can also be seen in dozens of reality shows in our culture in which people are searching for love, satisfaction and sexual fulfillment, such as *The Bachelor*, *The Bachelorette* and *For the Love of [fill in the celebrity's name]*. The plot of these shows usually goes as follows: The main character, who is either a famous celebrity or an attractive man or woman, gets a house filled with the most beautiful people the show's producers can find. Throughout the course of the show, the main character physically and emotionally "tests" each contestant in order to find out which one is his or her true love. After the individual gets down to two contestants through a series of eliminations, there is a season finale in which the main character picks the contestant he or she believes will be a true soul mate forever. But on the reunion show, which occurs about six months after the season finale, we find that the new couple has broken up, and the main character is now as empty and lonely as before.

I find it so crazy that even with the ability to choose from an endless amount of sexual partners, it seems as if people still end up miserable and unsatisfied. In his book *Love, Sex & Lasting Relationships*, Chip Ingram made a profound observation about this sexual dilemma:

Unfortunately, despite all the hype in magazines, movies, seminars, and books, for the most part people aren't doing very well when it comes to this area of their lives. The words divorce, breakup, wounds, baggage, ex-mate, and abuse are far too common in our vocabulary. Even in surviving marriages the atmosphere often reeks of unhappiness and disappointment. We long to love and we long to be loved, but we just don't know how to do it very well. And for all the open talks there are about sex today, sexuality still ranks as one of the persistent points of conflicts in most relationships.[4]

If movies, television, music, magazines, romance novels, friends and even our own feelings and opinions cannot give us the advice we need to experience true joy and sexual satisfaction, where else can we turn in order to find the answers?

The Instruction Manual

I once heard a friend of mine say that he wished he had an "easy button" for life, like those seen in technology commercials, so that whenever he had a problem, he could consult someone with expertise for help. Having an "easy button" for understanding new technologies is a great idea, but wouldn't it be better to have such a button for understanding sex, the oldest mystery in the world? What if we could simply press a button and have a one-on-one conversation with the creator of sex and ask Him to give us the basic rundown of how it really works? Through this conversation we could learn the secrets to experiencing sexual satisfaction without getting hurt in the process. We could finally find out whether sex is solely for pleasure, as the liberal sexologists say, or if it's only for procreation, as the conservative religious people say. Also, we could finally find out why nights of pleasure without commitment always lead to empty mornings of sadness and regret.

After I reached the breaking point on my sexual journey, I discovered that there was a way to consult the creator of sex and to find the answers that everyone has been searching for.

"How is this possible?" you might ask. By discovering the truth about sex from the creator of all things good Himself—God.

God and Sex = Good?

When some of you hear the words "God" and "sex" together, you begin to think of your Sunday school teacher who said, "Sex is nasty, evil and dirty, so save it for the one you love in marriage." If this is your experience, you probably don't expect the Bible's supposed prehistoric, unprogressive, bigoted, legalistic teachings about sex to provide any insight that could be applied to your life in the twenty-first century.

When I first thought of the ideas of God and sex together, the image that came to my mind was of a newly married Christian couple in a movie I saw during my freshman year of college. In the movie, instead of enjoying time with his wife on his honeymoon, the husband was too afraid to have sex with her because he thought,due to his hyperreligious upbringing, that sex was nasty and evil. So he spent a majority of the movie running away from his wife in fear that God would smite him for enjoying sex with her.

This movie as well as many others in Hollywood caused me to believe that anyone who learned about sex from a religious perspective, especially a Christian perspective, would have an ignorant and repressed sexuality. I thought that God and sex were like oil and water, so I believed that the only way to truly experience satisfaction was to separate sex from any spiritual connation.

Once again, I was wrong.

When I started investigating what God has to say about sex, my previous views that God and sex did not mix began to change. I found out that there was an entire book in the Bible called the Song of Solomon that describes the love and sexual relationship between a husband and wife as an amazing, godly experience. I also found a throwback *USA Today* article called "Aha! Call It the Revenge of the Church Ladies" by award-winning journalist William Mattox Jr. in which he discussed how Christian men and women were among some of the most sexually satisfied people in the world.[5] Mattox supported his claims through surveys done by the University of Chicago and Stanford University.

As I continued to read different articles and books and listen to different seminars and sermons about God and sex, I became fascinated. I could hardly believe that God—or people who understood sex from a biblical perspective—could have so much positive insight on the issue.

When I began to talk with married Christian men and women about their sexual satisfaction levels after following God's design for sex, I became convinced that everything I had read was true. There were too many compelling testimonies from both men and women who experienced deep levels of sexual satisfaction when they started to follow God's design for their sexuality. Slowly, as I applied these principles to my life, I went from sexual emptiness and frustration to sexual joy and satisfaction. It was as if a light had been illuminated in regard to my sexuality.

You don't have to go through the painful process I went through in order to find the secrets to experiencing true sexual joy and satisfaction. In the coming pages I'm going to tell you all that I've discovered about God's teachings on sex and sexuality. I'll tell you things about sex that psychologists say even most married people don't discover until at least a decade into their marriage. Instead of learning the hard way, you can learn the easy way, skipping the mornings of regrets and going straight to the life of fulfillment.

It's time to take the next leap of faith in this journey by investigating what God has to say about sex. You've already tried listening to everyone else and found that they don't have the answers you are looking for. You've tried listening to yourself and found that you don't have the answers you are looking for—as the old saying of Alcoholics Anonymous goes, "Your best thinking is what got you here." The least you can do now is listen to God and learn what He has to say on the issue.

You've got nothing to lose.

Reflection

- In your sexual discovery, how have you come to define sex—that is, the face (who you have sex with) and the place (what context you have sex in)?
- When you hear the words "God" and "sex" together, what thoughts come to your mind?
- Are you willing to take a leap of faith and investigate God's design for sex and sexuality?

Part 2

WHAT WE WERE NEVER TAUGHT ABOUT SEX

3

A Journey to the Very Beginning

ontrary to popular belief, God is not a cosmic killjoy when it comes to sex. God never says that sex is evil or disgusting, and He is not trying to ruin all our fun. Rather, God says that sex is good and should be enjoyable. God doesn't want to limit our sexual satisfaction; He wants to enhance it.

Where did I find all this information? Believe it or not, I found it from reading the Bible and studying God's teachings about sex.

God Loves Sex

In the book of Genesis, the Bible teaches that God created the whole world and everything in it and declared that it was all good. We also read that God created the first man and woman and that their names were Adam and Eve: "So God created man in his own image, in the image of God he created him; male and female he created them" (1:27).

God didn't create Adam and Eve because He was lonely, as if He were a teenage girl without a prom date desperately in need of a friend. God didn't create Adam and Eve because

He was desperate for praise and attention, as if He were the middle child in a family of seven. God didn't create Adam and Eve to begrudgingly serve Him, as if He were a power-hungry dictator looking for someone who would obey His burdensome commands. God created Adam and Eve to glorify Him and to enjoy His goodness and to enjoy others forever. God was a perfectly joyful, perfectly satisfied and perfectly loved being who simply wanted others to experience the eternal fulfillment that He experienced.

God created Adam and Eve to be different from each other but to have equal value, dignity, honor and respect. The two equal-but-unique genders were made to complement and work alongside one another in love and harmony. After God created Adam and Eve, He was delighted with His children and said that what He had made was "very good" (Gen 1:31).

God was very intentional about the way He designed His beloved children. He purposely and intently created everything about their anatomies. Their cells, skin, hands, feet and even their sex organs—every part of Adam and Eve's bodies—were given to them by God as gifts to be used for the enjoyment of His goodness and to help them experience intimacy with Him. James writes, "Every good gift and every perfect gift is from above, coming down from the Father of lights" (James 1:17).

Sex was not an accidental event that Adam and Eve discovered when God wasn't looking. Sex and all sexual desires were an original part of God's design for His creation: "God blessed them. And God said to them, 'Be fruitful and multiply and fill the earth'" (Gen. 1:28).

God made sex a pleasurable experience in order to show His creations that He is a loving Father who wants His children to experience love, pleasure, passion, intimacy, excitement and fulfillment. God made Adam and Eve whole sexual beings with healthy sexual desires and a passionate sex drive. Stephen Schwambach says, "Sex is too good to have just happened. It didn't evolve as the result of some cosmic accident. Something this exquisite had to have been lovingly, brilliantly, creatively designed."[1]

God created their individual sexualities as a way to reveal to Adam and Eve His love for deep intimate relationships and as a way for them to develop deep intimate relationships with one another. The act of sex was not only designed for recreation or procreation. Sex was created for oneness and intimacy within a marriage: "A man shall leave his father and his mother and hold fast to his wife, and they shall become one flesh. And the man and his wife were both naked and were not ashamed" (Gen. 2:24–25).

God created the covenant of marriage as a representation of the oneness that He experiences, since He exists in a Trinity: three distinct persons yet one God. Marriage represents the unification between a man and a woman in which the two become one: physically, emotionally and spiritually. Sex between Adam and his wife Eve was a perfect reflection of God's intimacy and oneness as well as an act of worship unto Him.

Soul Condoms

Being a loving and wise Father, God decided that all sexual actions were to be experienced only within the covenant of marriage for the well-being and the maximization of pleasure for His children. He wanted each person to be sexually intimate with only one person in his or her lifetime. God designed Adam to have sexual desires only for his wife Eve, and He designed Eve to have sexual desires only for her husband Adam. Eve was Adam's perfect standard of beauty, and Adam was Eve's perfect standard of beauty.

By giving His creation sexual guardrails, God protected Adam and Eve and future couples from other people breaking into their marital intimacy. There would be no envy, jealousy, lust, adultery or rape among any of God's people. God intended all the married men who would ever walk the earth to be intimate with their wives and perfectly satisfied sexually and all the married women to be intimate with their husbands and perfectly satisfied sexually.

In First Corinthians, Paul writes, "The husband should fulfill his wife's sexual needs, and the wife should fulfill her husband's needs" (7:3, NLT). Sex wasn't created so that Adam could treat Eve as an object whose sole purpose in life was to satisfy his sexual appetite. Nor was sex created for Eve to lord it over Adam in order to control him and make him obey her bidding. Sex was a gift that Adam and Eve were to use to love, care for, serve, honor and enjoy one another in their marriage.

In his book *A Celebration of Sex*, Dr. Douglas Rosenau gives a perfect description of the sexual relationship of Adam and Eve in the garden of Eden: "They revealed a childlike trust and curiosity—laughing, exploring, giving and receiving love. Sex was a glorious, innocent celebration lived out with instinctual honesty, respect, and zest for life. It was naked and unashamed with no performance, anxiety, inhibitions, pain, or selfish skillful deficits."[2]

Our Desire for Intimacy

As I started researching the root of my sexual desires, I discovered that it wasn't crazy, wild, random sex that I truly desired. What I really longed for was to experience true intimacy in a committed relationship with someone who loved me—more than experiencing mere sexual pleasure.

I wanted someone in my life with whom I could be vulnerable and not fear that she would hurt me. I wanted someone in my life with whom I could be naked and not feel ashamed; a person who would be satisfied with me physically, emotionally and spiritually; someone who would not desire any other but me. I wanted a person with whom I could actually be myself without fearing that she would make a run for the woods. I wanted to experience sex full of passion and love but without any shame and guilt. I may be wrong, but I believe that if you dig deep into the desires of your heart, you will find that you too long for this kind of committed, intimate relationship.

The reason we have these desires for a committed, intimate sexual relationship is that God's design for sex and intimacy is embedded in the very fabric of our being. This kind of intimacy can only be experienced between a man and a woman in a committed, intimate relationship—that is, in the context of marriage.

Oddly enough, the idea of being satisfied sexually and emotionally in a committed intimate relationship is understood in our culture, which can be seen in the plot of most romantic comedies.

Take for example the 2011 movie *No Strings Attached.* Adam (your typical male bachelor) and his best friend Emma (your typical single girl who is afraid of love due to previous heartbreak) decide to use one another only for sex as nothing more than casual sexual partners. For a while they are able to do so, but eventually they develop feelings for one another. After trying to fight their feelings through most of the movie, the story ends with Adam and Emma confessing their love for one another and beginning an exclusive relationship together.

This same story line can be seen in *Friends with Benefits.* Dylan and Jamie come to the mutual conclusion that sex should not come with any emotional attachments, so they agree to engage in a sexual relationship with one another without any commitment involved. After a period of time, however, they realize that casual sex cannot work. They end their relationship, but a series of events bring the two back together, and the movie ends with Dylan and Jamie sharing a passionate kiss and starting a relationship.

As we can see from these movies, even our hypersexual culture understands that true satisfaction can only come from a committed, intimate relationship.

Still not convinced?

Take a look at the life of Fabio Lanzoni (known simply as Fabio), the Italian fashion model and international sex symbol who captured the hearts of millions of women around the world in the 1990s. All his life Fabio has been surrounded by oceans of beautiful women who effortlessly throw themselves at him at the sight of his million-dollar smile. At the pinnacle of his career, he had his pick of thousands of women. I can only imagine that the number of his sexual exploits would put even the legendary Don Juan to shame.

Yet in a 2013 interview on Oprah's show *Oprah: Where Are They Now?* The fifty-four-year-old Fabio, who has never been married, opened up about his love life.

He tells about how he messed up by letting the love of his life go when he was younger. He described the woman as one who had showed him the kind of unconditional love that everyone desires to experience. Yet being young and naïve at the time, Fabio had believed that relationships and sex with other women would bring him true satisfaction and joy. But they didn't.

"That's the biggest lesson God taught me. When you have love in your life, you have happiness, you have everything,"

Fabio said in his interview. "When you don't have love, you can have all the money [success] in the world, and you're nothing." Fabio went on to say that he had no interest in having any more affairs (cheap, meaningless sexual relationships) because he'd had a lot of them in his past and they had never satisfied him.

Now, Fabio said, after being with maybe hundreds of women, he was ready to get married and to begin an exclusive intimate relationship because he finally understood that this would truly satisfy the desire of his heart.[3]

Real Intimacy

As we previously read in Genesis 2:25, in the garden Adam and Eve were naked and not ashamed. This is the perfect example of what I mean by real intimacy. Dr. Ted Roberts says that intimacy is not about being comfortable and close to the perfect person of your dreams. Rather, "intimacy is being uncomfortably close and exposed to another imperfect person."[4]

When two people experience real intimacy, they stand before each other and say, "I am not going to hide anything from you. I am going to show you all my fears, secrets, dreams, failures, goals, hopes and shortcomings related to my past, present and future because I trust you and know that you are committed to my well-being." Real intimacy is founded on deep security, trust, honor, love and commitment in a relationship, which are fully expressed between a man and a woman in marriage.

The desire to experience real intimacy is why people are so obsessed with sex. It's because sex is the greatest physical representation of real intimacy between a man and a woman.

Let me explain.

In God's perfect design, when a husband and a wife who love each other have sex, two important things happen. First, they get naked before each other, and second, they enter into one another (intercourse). The nakedness is symbolic of being vulnerable, showing the most private and intimate part of ourselves to someone else and not being ashamed. It is a representation of our desire to be known, loved and accepted just the way we are by another person. The entering into one another is symbolic of our need for close intimate bonding. While we want to be accepted just the way we are, we also desperately long for a person who will not only see us for our true self but will also want to connect with and be committed to us unconditionally for the rest of our lives.

Everything Had to Go Wrong

God's design for committed, intimate relationships was His design for all the men and women who would ever walk the earth. Everyone was to be happy, joyful, content and satisfied first in God, their loving Father, and then in their spouses. Men would use sex only as an act of service to satisfy their wives, and women would use sex only as an act of service to satisfy their husbands: "May your fountain be blessed, and may you rejoice in the wife of your youth. A loving doe, a graceful deer— may her breasts satisfy you always, may you ever be intoxicated with her love." (Prov. 5:18–19, NIV).

Things were this way until sin entered the world and made everything go wrong.

When sin entered the world, it destroyed every part of God's creation. God's perfect creation became imperfect as people turned away from Him in an attempt to satisfy their desires on their own.

The entering of sin into the world is known as the Fall. In the Fall, Adam and his wife Eve ate the forbidden fruit from the

Tree of the Knowledge of Good and Evil and turned away from God's perfect plan for their lives (see Gen. 3:1–7). Adam and Eve didn't trust God and felt as if they knew better than God. When they sinned and ate the fruit, they made a bold statement to God, their loving Father, by subconsciously saying, "Dad, I know that You designed us to be perfectly satisfied with all that You have given us to enjoy. But we don't want to follow Your ways. Instead, we're going to act upon our own feelings and desires by doing whatever we feel would be pleasing to our own bodies, even if You tell us that's wrong. We're going to live our lives our way, based on how we feel, and we believe that we know what will satisfy us better than You do."

Adam and Eve quickly regretted their decision, just as we do after we make mistakes in our lives. The same fruit that they believed would give them joy and satisfaction was the very object that ruined their lives. Adam and Eve's sin not only corrupted every part of the created order, but it also fractured their souls, and when they reproduced, they created a race of people with broken souls who were no longer physically, emotionally, spiritually or sexually whole.

Soul Fractures

After diving deeper into the story of Adam and Eve, I came to realize that the source of my sexual dilemma wasn't simply limited to poor sexual decisions that I'd made. There was a deeper issue beyond the surface—a brokenness in my soul. As difficult as it is to say, especially as a man, I realized that I am someone who is hurting and is looking for anything and anyone that will make me whole again. We all are. This brokenness affects everything about our anatomy: our physical, emotional, spiritual and sexual natures. Let me explain.

First, our brokenness affects us physically, because we will experience a physical death in this life, which was not part of God's plan. God promised that if mankind were to sin against Him, they would surely die (see Gen. 2:17), which shows that death wasn't part of His original design. This promise didn't result in an immediate physical death (even though physical death was part of it) but in a spiritual death that occurred over time. Also, our bodies now experience disease, birth defects and a variety of illnesses as physical effects of the Fall. Our physical bodies are broken in ways that science, medicine and doctors can't seem to find solutions for.

Next, our brokenness affects us emotionally, because we now have unstable emotions that are unable to remain healthy, leading to the many defects of the human mind. Illnesses such as ADHD, autism, bipolar disorder and depression have plagued us or those we love. We also are unable to establish healthy relationships with others. Broken friendships, devastated marriages and feuding families are the results of our emotional brokenness that psychologists and self-help books can't ultimately provide solutions for.

Third, our brokenness affects us spiritually. As we can tell from the disastrous state of our planet, there is a severed relationship between humankind and our creator. We are spiritually separated from the God who created us (see Isa. 59:2). Many people are aware of this spiritual brokenness and attempt to fill the gap between us and God with yoga and New Age spirituality. Unfortunately, these methods can't provide solutions to our problems. We can't build a bridge back to God with our religious actions alone, and we are as distant from God today as we were in our past.

Selfish Sexuality

Since our sexuality is made up of our physical, emotional and spiritual natures, we can see how all the other forms of brokenness lead us to a broken sexual condition as well. Due to our brokenness, we are no longer sexually whole beings who trust God with our sexuality. There is a void in our lives that we are trying to fill, and we are willing to use any means to fill that void.

Young women don't sleep around simply to feel a sense of sexual liberation or to enjoy uncontrolled sexual desires; it's because they are trying to use sex to fill a void in their souls. Young men don't sleep around simply because they are highly evolved primates who always think about sex; it's because they are looking for any feeling that will satisfy and ease the brokenness they experience in their lives.

Unfortunately, all our means of achieving sexual satisfaction do not work, because we are so consumed with the temporary pleasures of right now that we don't take into account the fact that the long-term effects of our actions will never satisfy us. If our sexuality is solely focused on me, myself and I rather than on God, others and real intimacy, we will never experience the true joy and sexual satisfaction that we desire.

There Is Hope

The good news is that God is not an impassive, uncaring creator, as some have falsely labeled Him. He is not some deadbeat father who drops his kids off in the street and asks them to fend for themselves. God has not left us in a continual state of selfishness, brokenness and emptiness. As a loving Father, He is conscious of our troubles and desires to give us hope and healing. God wants to guide us on a journey so that we can become sexually whole again and experience true sexual joy and satisfaction that comes from real intimacy.

This news should be a blessing for everyone. I know it was for me the moment I heard about it. I felt as if a weight had been lifted off my chest when I found out that I was not alone and that everyone makes mistakes and has sexual regrets. While no one is perfect and we all fall short (see Rom. 3:23), we can achieve satisfaction in true intimacy regardless of our sexual history and the mistakes we have made in our past.

Am I Selfish?

The first step to overcoming our problem is to admit that there is a problem, which as a man has been extremely hard for me to do. I've had to learn that if I don't fully know what my problem is, I won't admit that I have a problem. It was only when I realized how my sexuality was selfish (all about me, myself and I) and in the way of my achieving true sexual joy and satisfaction that I was able to begin the journey to experience true sexual joy and satisfaction.

At first I didn't believe that my sexuality was selfish, and especially not that it was sinful, because I didn't have a good understanding of sin or selfishness. I thought of sin as an act that was destructive, violent, wicked, vile and malicious. When I looked at my sexuality and didn't see it as violent or destructive, I didn't believe that it was sinful. When I thought of selfishness, I thought of doing something that didn't take others into consideration. Since I didn't see that my sexuality was entirely inconsiderate, because the women I slept with enjoyed it too, I did not see it as selfish.

Yet I was missing the whole point, because sin isn't always something that is violent or malicious. Sin is believing that our own ways rather than God's ways will satisfy us. This idea relates to selfishness, which I have heard defined as being concerned chiefly with one's own personal profit or pleasure while disregarding that of others.

As you can see, the definition for sin is interconnected with the definition for selfishness. When we sin, we are selfish toward God and fail to believe that He is a good Father whose ways are best since we're only concerned with our own personal feeling and pleasure. We don't view God as a good Father who wants us to experience any enjoyment; we view Him as a liar and an obstacle to achieving true sexual joy and satisfaction on our own terms.

When I started talking to more of my friends about this idea, I discovered that at the core of their sexuality and sexual decisions, most people were like I had been: they did not believe in their hearts that God knew what was best in their lives—even though they would never say it out loud.

But, as we'll discover in the next chapter, selfishness is our main obstacle to achieving true sexual joy and satisfaction.

Reflection

- How do you feel after learning about God's design for sex and sexuality?
- Would you say that real intimacy is something that you desire?
- Do you feel that you are a whole person, or do you think something is missing in your life?

4

It's All about Me

Back in my nonstop partying days in college, the song notoriously known for getting things started was "Every Girl in the World" by Young Money. As advertised by the title, the song told the story of everyone in the band desiring to have sex with every girl in the world. The song was a club banger, an instant success as it reached its peak position on the charts as the number ten song on the US Billboard Hot 100.

If you were to tell your grandma about the song's success, she would probably ask how in the world it was possible that a song with such lewd, misogynistic lyrics could be loved by so many. The answer is obvious. The lyrics gave a perfect diagnosis of the selfish sexual desires of most young men in our culture (including me at the time): to experience sexual satisfaction by using women as sheer objects.

When I took a closer look at the song's lyrics, I realized how it diagnosed Young Money (and me) as not viewing women as created beings who had been made in the image and likeness of God. We did not view these women as somebody's sister, daughter or mother. We did not view these women as people who had real souls with real feelings, emotions and desires. We did not view these women as individuals who had dreams to be loved and valued by a man, not just to be used and discarded as if they were disposable utensils. Put bluntly, women to us were only meaningless, objectified tools whose task was simply to bring us sexual pleasure.

Sadly, this is the issue with being selfish: it caves our soul inward and causes us to focus solely on pleasing and satisfying ourselves instead of God and others.

The Desire Is Not the Problem

In order to make sure that no one misinterprets what I say in this chapter, let me make something very clear. God made both men and women to be sexual beings, so I am not saying that there is something inherently selfish, sinful or evil with people having sexual desires.

When I use the phrase "selfish sexuality," what I mean is that we don't see sex as a gift that God has given us to enjoy within marriage; rather we see sex as an act, the sole purpose of which is to satisfy and bring pleasure to me, myself and I. Our sexual desires become selfish when we willfully attach them to people whom God has told us not to. The selfish sexual desire is what the Bible calls lust, which I once heard defined as "having normal sexual desires with selfishness."[1] This lingering lust problem, which originated in the garden of Eden, is the main obstacle that gets in the way of our experiencing true sexual joy and satisfaction.

As I describe different categories of selfish sexuality in this chapter, our focus should be on the desire at the root of the action rather than on any particular action. While the action is part of the problem, it's only a symptom and not the root. Every action begins as a thought, and every thought comes from the broken soul of the individual, which is longing to be satisfied with something outside the will of God.

I know that some of you may disagree with certain things and be tempted to put down this book during this chapter, but I hope that you remain patient and bear with me. I understand that the cardinal evil in the eyes of today's generation is condemning others by saying that they are wrong. With catchy slogans such as "follow your heart" and "YOLO" ("you only live once") to be found everywhere, it only make sense that self-autonomy is the chief end of human life for most of us today. But we have to be careful, because "there is a way that seems right to a man, but its end is the way to death" (Prov. 14:12). So I ask you to trust me. My goal in this chapter is not to point the finger at others in order to show what is wrong with everyone else. My sole desire is to bring a brief, healthy diagnosis to a problem that we all, especially myself, deal with and to point us to a long-lasting solution.

Selfish Sexuality: Heterosexual Desires

As stated in the previous chapter, when I started learning about God's sexual design, I discovered that God's original plan for men and women was to be satisfied with the heterosexual spouses He had provided for them. A person's spouse was supposed to be his or her standard of beauty and the only person with whom he or she would experience sexual longings, sexual intimacy and sexual satisfaction. But due to the Fall, everyone's sexuality was broken, which caused us to become selfish individuals who disregard God's design for sex and sexuality in pursuit of our own personal definition and fulfillment.

My life was a perfect example of the first type of selfish sexuality that I'll describe: the selfish heterosexual desire.

A person who has a selfish heterosexual desire believes that he or she can be satisfied by engaging in sexual actions with someone of the opposite sex who is not his or her spouse. When I say that a person has selfish heterosexual desires, I don't mean that a person merely notices the beauty or attractiveness of an individual of the opposite sex, because there is nothing wrong with someone admiring the beauty of God's creation. Neither am I saying that it's wrong for a person (a single person, that is) to show romantic affection or to enjoy romantic affection from people to whom he or she is not married. What I am describing is people who have intentional sexual fantasies, unrelenting sexual desires and unhealthy sexual craving toward an individual of the opposite sex to whom they are not married that leads them to act out on those desires.

I have seen a selfish heterosexual desire fleshed out in four basic ways.

2-D Sex. One of the most common ways in which I saw my college friends attempt to satisfy their sexual desires was through Internet pornography. Pornography is defined as "any written or visual medium [books, magazines, videos, television, movies, the Internet] that displays nudity or sexual activity that excites sexual feelings. It is believed that 90 percent of people have watched pornography before the age of sixteen.[2]

Pornography feeds directly to the desires of a selfish sexuality because it allows people to physically gratify the desires of their hearts, and this causes their sexual fantasies to become a 2-D reality. Though pornography seems to meet an individual's immediate desire for sexual pleasure, it never satisfies a person's soul, because it only adds fuel to the burning desires of lust, which always keeps its viewers coming back for more.

I could write this entire book based on my firsthand

experiences alone about how selfish, unsatisfying and destructive pornography is, but I don't want to detract from the main point. However, if I were to give one reason that porn is dangerous and hurtful, I would have to paraphrase words said by Pope John Paul that have resonated with my soul: The main issue with pornography is that it doesn't show enough of the person—it doesn't reveal that he or she is a person made in the image of God.[3]

In other words, God desires everyone to treat people the way that they themselves desire to be treated, and what porn does is dehumanize men and women as sheer sexual tools meant to satisfy our own selfish gratification—something no one desires to experience.

Couples with Benefits. Instead of following God's design for marital sexual intimacy, some choose to have sex with those they are in a dating relationship with, cohabitating with or engaged to. This is probably the most difficult type of sex to diagnose as selfish, because most will say, "We are not harming anyone; we are consenting adults. We are 'in love,' and God is love."

To the modern mind the idea of two "committed" people who care about each other having sex makes perfect sense. Yet the problem is that this sexual definition is based upon personal feelings and not on the Word of God. When people who are not married have sex, they hurt God by disregarding His design for a design of their own. Also, they hurt each other because they lead one another into sexual activities that have been prohibited by God.

People who have sex while they are dating, engaged or co-habitating may think that it is OK because they say they love each other, but if we take a close look at their actions, we realize that they really don't love one another. In the Bible it says that love does not delight in evil (see 1 Cor. 13:6). If two people really love one another, they will do things that push one another toward God instead of ones that push each other away from God. Yes, God is love, but two people intentionally leading each other away from God is one of the most unloving acts they can do.

No Strings Attached. There are people who will have sex with anyone of the opposite gender, whether they are in an exclusive dating relationship with a person or not. Similar to those practicing other kinds of selfish sex, they believe that having sex with someone without being married will satisfy them; unfortunately, it won't. Sex without lifelong marital commitment and love between two partners is unfulfilling sex.

People who have casual sex end up treating others as if they are simply bodies to be used for their own personal pleasure instead of souls to be loved for the person's benefit. Though some psychologists would say that sexual liberty (the freedom to make any sexual decision one chooses) is at the core of American liberty and that restricting anyone's sexual choices is as evil an act as restricting a person of his right to vote, they do not take God into the equation. God isn't some impassive, licentious father who allows his children to engage in any hurtful action they please without ever caring about their well-being. God is a loving Father who wants His children to experience life abundantly while making sexually healthy decisions that lead to life, joy and satisfaction—which can only be experienced in marriage.

True sexual liberty isn't the ability to make any sexual decision one chooses, because in reality, making carefree, unhealthy sexual decisions is really selective sexual slavery. True sexual liberty is the freedom to make any healthy sexual decision that glorifies God, blesses another and respects oneself.

Rolling Stones. Studies show that 41 percent of marriages have at least one or both spouses who admitted to committing either a physical or emotional affair (adultery).[4] Due to the effects of the Fall, everyone experiences a selfish sexuality, even those who are happily married. While some people stay faithful to their spouses, others don't and act upon their desires by engaging in extramarital sex. After hearing adultery stories from close friends of mine who had committed the act, I found out that having an affair has nothing to do with the love, or lack of love, that a person has for his or her spouse. As with any sexual sin, at the root of adultery is a heart that's concerned only with satisfying oneself regardless of the consequences.

Also, contrary to popular belief, a selfish sexuality won't disappear when a person gets married. Instead, it will continue to be present and, if left unchecked, will grow more selfish along with the difficulties of marriage.

If God simply defined sex as something to be experienced between two people who love each other, what happens when a husband doesn't love his wife anymore? What if he chooses to love his secretary instead? Does that mean he should have an affair with his secretary and leave his wife simply because he is a consenting adult who is in love? Of course not. Love isn't simply a feeling to be experienced but a lifelong commitment that is made.

The root problem with a person who engages in a selfish heterosexual desire is the statement they make to God by indirectly saying, "God, I know that You designed men and women to be sexually satisfied with their spouses, but I don't want to follow Your design. Instead, I am going to act upon my own will by following my sexual desires and engaging in sex with whomever I please. I am going to live my life according to the way I feel.

And I believe that living the way I feel will make me happy. My way is better than Your way, and I am going to do what I feel is best—regardless of what You've said."

Selfish Sexuality: Homosexual Desires

Before I describe this next category of selfish sexuality—homosexual desire—I want to reiterate a point that I stated earlier: all forms of selfish sexualities are the same.

Contrary to what some religions or churches might teach, there is no form of sexual sin that is superior to the other—they are all equal. One is not a varsity-level sin and the other a junior-varsity-level sin. Homosexual desire is one form of a selfish sexuality, just as selfish heterosexual desire is a form of a selfish sexuality.

As I said about pornography, I would need to write a separate book to fully explain the complexity of homosexual desire (a book I don't believe I am competent to write); therefore, I will give only a brief, broad definition and understanding of homosexuality for the purpose of our current discussion.

Before I address this issue, I can only imagine the myriad of negative reactions that some people have toward a Christian view of homosexuality. "Bigots," "unloving," "evil" and "oppressors" are a few words that may come to people's mind. But please don't put the book down without looking at the whole picture.

Never does God say that it's wrong for a man or a woman to desire to be loved. Never does God say that it's wrong for a man or a woman to desire to be loved by another person. Never does God say that it's wrong for a man to love another man or for a woman to love another woman. When asked what the greatest commandment was, Jesus said that it was to love one another the way we ourselves would want to be loved (see Matt. 22:39).

Yet God said that all romantic and sexual feelings should be experienced with someone of the opposite sex (see Gen. 2:24). Love isn't defined by our personal feelings and opinions, as I stated in the section about sex outside heterosexual marriage; love is defined by God's Word.

It wasn't until I was able to listen and learn from a good friend of mine who experiences homosexual feelings that I truly came to understand this desire better. My friend told me that although those who have homosexual desires feel as though their sexual desires will be satisfied by engaging in sexual actions with individuals of the same gender, they are no different from heterosexual people. Similar to how I experience sexual desires for those of the opposite sex to whom I am not married, which is not from God but from self, those who experience homosexual desires have them toward people of the same sex, which is also not from God but from self.

Similar to myself or anyone else with selfish sexuality, some people act on their homosexual desires, and others don't. But once again, the action is not the main problem or the root of the problem—though the action is still problematic. The root issue is with the motive behind the action, which is a heart that believes that it can be sexually satisfied by doing something outside the will of God.

The problem at the root of homosexual desire is the same as the problem at the root of selfish heterosexual desire, which is the statement it makes toward God by indirectly saying, "God, even though I know that You designed men and women to be sexually satisfied with their heterosexual spouses, I don't want to follow Your design. Instead, I am going to act upon my own personal feelings by having sex or sexual desires for people of the same sex. I am going live my life according to the way I feel, and I believe that living the way I feel will satisfy me and make me happy. My way is better than Your way, and I'm going to do what I feel is best—regardless of what You've said."

I know that this section may be extremely difficult for some to accept, but please hear me out. If God is a good Father who not only wants the best for all His children but who also knows what is best for all His children, we need to trust His design for sex and relationships regardless of our feelings and emotions, because only He know what will truly satisfy the desires of our souls.

Selfish Sexuality: Nonhuman Sexual Desires

This last category of selfish sexuality is not as common among my friends or the people I have talked to, and a majority of those reading this book probably will never experience this type of desire. Even though cases of nonhuman sexual desire are extremely rare, I decided to include it in this section, because it gives a better look at what it really means for us to have a selfish sexuality.

The last category of selfish sexuality is nonhuman sexual desires. People with nonhuman sexual desire try to be sexually satisfied by using objects that are not human to experience sexual pleasure or satisfaction (blow-up dolls, vibrators or any other inanimate object).

Even though the following story sounds pretty weird, I saw an example of this desire in an article that I read about the 2010 wedding of a twenty-eight-year-old Korean man who married his body pillow in an official ceremony (true story).[5] Most of us will laugh at someone like this and say, "This guy is mentally insane. Does he really believe that a body pillow will satisfy him?" The ironic thing about that statement is that God says the same exact thing to all of us when we believe that we can be satisfied by engaging in any sexual action outside His will.

As a loving Father, God looks upon us with a saddened heart as we seek meaning and love from things that could never fulfill us. Though He wants us to feast and be satisfied with the banquet of righteousness—which is sex in the context of marriage—we often choose to dig through the trash and feed off the breadcrumbs of immorality—which is sex outside the context of marriage. To put it simply, it breaks God's heart when we don't trust Him for knowing what is best in our life.

Sexual Transformation

When I first saw how I had disregarded God's design for my sexuality in pursuit of my own personal happiness, I assumed that the decisions I'd made were so terrible that God would never forgive me. I began to think that because I was no longer a virgin and had messed up in my past, I was damaged sexual goods with no hope of experiencing real intimacy. But then I learned that this was not true.

While every one of us has sinned and turned away from God's design for sexuality in pursuit of our own, God has never—and will never—give up on us. God is a loving Father who always wants His children to come back and be with Him, no matter what they have done. He is willing to forgive us, heal us, make us clean and provide us with a whole sexuality. Realizing that we've moved far from God shouldn't make us run further away from Him. Instead, it should compel us to cry to Him for help.

We can become sexually whole again. Regardless of the category of selfish sexuality that we have fallen into, and no matter what we have done sexually in our past, God can supernaturally transform our life and allow us to experience true sexual joy and satisfaction.

Reflection

- Which form of selfish sexuality would you relate to the most?
- Do you feel that your current form of sexuality is beneficial to your life? Why or why not?
- Do you believe that God is a good Father who truly cares about your joy and well-being? On what do you base your belief?

5

Healing and a Fresh New Start

One of my favorite stories in the Bible, a story that many of us probably have heard dozens of times, is the parable of the prodigal son in Luke 15. This parable is arguably Jesus' most famous parable and one of the most beloved stories in literature. Jesus tells this story in order to describe God's unconditional love and forgiveness for all His people. If we take a deeper look into the plot of the parable, we can see how the story of the son is identical to our sexual journey.

Jesus begins the parable by telling of a man and his two sons. The man is an honest worker and a loving father who does all he can to care for and provide for his sons. One day the youngest son comes to his father and asks for his share of the inheritance. By doing this, the son was telling his father that he was dead to him, because children in ancient cultures got their inheritance only when their parents had died. Upon hearing his son's request, the father, certainly brokenhearted, complies and gives his son his share of the inheritance, and the son goes on his way.

After leaving his father's home, the son goes to a foreign town and spends all his money on reckless living in an attempt to satisfy his own desires. Since he finally has the freedom to do as he pleases, he begins to indulge in his selfish sexuality by having sex with countless prostitutes.

Then, out of nowhere, a famine enters the land and causes the son to lose everything. All the money, friends, women, sex and pleasure he has obtained are gone. In the blink of an eye, he goes from nights of passion and ecstasy to days of emptiness and misery.

The son becomes so poor and downtrodden that in order to feed himself he finds a job taking care of pigs. Unfortunately, the money he receives isn't enough to buy food. With no one to offer him a helping hand, the son is forced to stoop so low as to want to eat the same slop he serves the pigs.

After finally hitting rock bottom, the son comes to his senses and realizes how foolish he is. Instead of eating pig slop and wasting away in misery, the son decides to go back home to the love of his father, hoping that if he asks for forgiveness, his father might take him back as a mere servant.

As the son nears home, the father sees him from a long way off and feels compassion for him. He sprints to his son, embraces him and begins to kiss him in joy. Immediately the son begins to apologize for everything he has done; he humbly begs the father to allow him to stay and asks if he may work as a servant in the house.

Out of joy for his son's return, the father calls for a huge celebration. He clothes his son in his best robes and gives him a fine ring. The father doesn't attack his son by reminding him of all the bad decisions he's made. He isn't disgusted because his son has had sex before marriage. He forgives his son and welcomes him back with open arms as a loving father would.

This story is a beautiful picture of the love and forgiveness that God shows for all those who come back to Him. Just like the son in the story, we tell our Father—God—that we don't need Him because we want to live our lives however we want. We embrace our own design for sex and love and live recklessly to some degree, because we believe that doing so will satisfy our desires. Eventually, after going through a roller coaster of emotions, we hit rock bottom and realize that our way of life isn't satisfying us. That's when we begin to turn and feel our way to God (see Acts 17:27).

The moment that we take those initial steps back toward God, He runs toward us and embraces us just as the father in the story did his son. God doesn't tell us how disappointed He is because of all the bad decisions we've made. Neither does He say that we are too filthy and sinful because of our past sexual experiences. He immediately forgives us and covers us with His grace and love. He calls us His beloved children and promises to heal us and make us whole again.

Firsthand Transformation Experience

Some of you may think that I am suggesting a type of super-spiritual idealism, but trust me, I'm not. This parable isn't just some story that a poor Jewish carpenter called Jesus told two thousand years ago; it's the testimony of my life.

During my teenage years I lived a sexually selfish lifestyle in which I was concerned only with satisfying my own desires. I spent hours lusting after the girls in my classroom and after women I saw on television and on the Internet, which led to my strong addiction to pornography.

While I was at college, I acted upon my desires by having sexual relationships with any woman who was willing, and I viewed sex as a sport in which I competed with my football teammates and friends in order to prove that I was a man. I didn't care about God and His design for sex and sexuality. It was my life, and I was going to live it any way I pleased. I didn't care about all the people I hurt or the girls' hearts I broke. Because I was so selfish, I never had a serious relationship—I simply went from girl to girl, manipulating each one by giving them temporary affection just so I could add a notch to my proverbial belt. I was only living for myself, but this selfish lifestyle left me empty and miserable.

Something happened during my sophomore year that caused everything to change. I was invited to a Bible study by one of my football teammates, and it was there that I met the guy who would become my mentor, Zach.

Before he taught me about God's design for sex, Zach first introduced me to Jesus. He introduced me to a God who loved me so much that He would step down into human history to live the life I couldn't live and die the death I deserved. He introduced me to a God who knew all the wrong that I had done in my past but was still willing to love me, forgive me and accept me as His beloved son. He introduced me to a God who deeply desired to heal my broken soul and satisfy the desires of my heart.

Through the Bible studies I had with Zach, I learned that I couldn't do anything to fix myself or get right with God on my own. I needed to repent of my sins and trust in Jesus, because He was the only One who could provide salvation and life transformation. Zach told me that God's gift of grace didn't come from doing good deeds in an effort to earn God's favor but through accepting the good deed that God did for us through the life, death and resurrection of Jesus Christ.

After wrestling with the teachings of the Bible study for weeks and after a lot of second-guessing myself, I eventually decided that it was time to give my life to Christ. I came to the realization that if I continued to take my own path in life, I would destroy my chance of having a real relationship with God and also ruin any hopes of experiencing true love in the future. I knew that I needed Jesus to heal my soul and give me a new life. I needed a fresh new start, and I was ready to surrender everything to God.

Through the grace of Jesus Christ, God renewed my soul, and I received healing for my brokenness. Upon trusting in Christ, God came into my life and transformed me into a new creation. I was no longer a slave who was forced to obey his selfish sexual passions and desires. I was now a sexually whole man who was free to follow God's will for my life and experience true joy and satisfaction.

Second Corinthians says, "If anyone is in Christ, he is a new creation. The old has passed away; behold, the new has come" (5:17). This transformation and wholeness is not only something God did for me, but it's something that He can do for everyone who gives their life to Him by having faith in Jesus Christ as their Savior and Lord.

The Reset Button

When most people hear about the gospel of Jesus Christ, they merely think about souls being saved from an eternity in hell, but they forget about the gospel's power to supernaturally transform lives. Also, most people live with the idea that eternal life is something a person begins experiencing upon death, but that is not true. Eternal life begins the moment we trust in Jesus.

Jesus promised to send the Holy Spirit, the third person of the Trinity, into the lives of those who believe and put their faith in Him. The Holy Spirit comes into our souls to wash, cleanse, sanctify and heal us and to make us whole. If we desire to experience true sexual joy and satisfaction, we must first surrender our life and sexuality to God so that we can begin whatever healing process we may need to go through.

Jesus is here to help us start over and to experience sexual wholeness. There is a God who passionately, gracefully, lovingly, continually and relentlessly pursues us and cares for us. As a loving Father, He wants to take us on a journey so that we can experience sexual wholeness and satisfaction.

Dr. Mark Laaser says,

> The healing journey is a constant challenge to trust God more. The process of true change is achieved only as we die to ourselves, relinquish our fears and doubts, depend more on Christ and surrender to him. As we practice this more and more, God leads us continually away from sinful old behaviors—sexual ones and others—toward new behaviors that are pure, healthy, and life-giving.[1]

So what are you waiting for? It's time to begin the healing process and to continue the journey to experiencing true sexual joy and satisfaction. There isn't a special prayer that you have to say in order to receive salvation and transformation. All you have to do is confess your sins to God, repent, ask for forgiveness and commit your life and sexuality to Jesus.

> Do not be deceived: neither the sexually immoral, nor idolaters, nor adulterers, nor men who practice homosexuality, nor thieves, nor the greedy, nor drunkards, nor revilers, nor swindlers will inherit the kingdom of God. *And such were some of you.* But you were washed, you were sanctified, you were justified in the name of the Lord Jesus Christ and by the Spirit of our God. (1 Cor. 6:9–11)

Reflection

- What part of your sexual past do you think God won't forgive?
- Do you desire to experience sexual transformation through Christ?
- If God desires to love and transform you, what is holding you back from giving your life and sexuality fully to Him?

Part 3
How to Experience a Healthy, Whole Sexuality

6

The Secrets to Becoming a Great Lover

To say that following God's design for sex and sexuality was a walk in the park after I became a Christian would be to lie. For months my nights were filled with anger, fear, tears, pain, regrets, mistakes and compromise as I struggled with believing that I could experience a righteous sexual future after living an immoral sexual past.

As I became more transparent and comfortable sharing my difficulties with others, I found out that I wasn't alone. All my close friends were finding it impossible to live according to God's sexual standards, and since I was the only one who wasn't still sleeping around, watching porn or masturbating, people turned to me for advice about their sexual struggles.

Throughout college I received so many random sexual questions that at times I felt as if I was a talk-radio-show host. From having to convince a girl that her boyfriend shouldn't go to the strip club for his bachelor party to explaining to my best friend that a threesome for his five-year-marriage anniversary was not a good idea, you name the question, I got it.

Though I was trying my best to follow God's design for sex and to encourage others to do the same, I couldn't find any good resources about sex and singleness that my friends and I would actually read, because all the books I came across were either pitifully irrelevant or dreadfully boring. All this led me to start my own website, *The Urban Gospel Mission*, with the purpose of writing articles addressing the topic of sex and many other taboo issues in order to encourage my friends to stay faithful to God.

Eventually, after writing a few articles and receiving some good feedback from others, I started to contemplate writing a book about single sexuality. Though I was extremely insecure and did not want to do it, since I felt unqualified, I also felt that such a book needed to be written not by some expert or scholar but by a regular person who could relate firsthand to the everyday struggles of singles.

So once I decided to write the book, I knew that I needed to be extremely knowledgeable about the subject matter in order to provide a real impact on the lives of those who would read it. After reading dozens of Christian books about sex and relationships, I stumbled upon one that was written specifically to young single adults, *Soul Virgins* by sex therapist Dr. Doug Rosenau and counselor Michael Todd Wilson.

I was so impacted by *Soul Virgins* that I decided to reach out to Dr. Doug personally in order to learn more about sex from a biblical perspective. As I looked up his information online, I discovered that he lived not only in the same state but also in the same county in which I lived.

At our first meeting I discovered a warm, loving and welcoming personality in Dr. Doug. He was extremely excited that I was writing a book about sex for young adults and was willing to help me through the process. Even though he had a busy schedule, he penciled in time for me to come into his office the following week to talk about my book. With more than thirty years of sex therapy under his belt, Dr. Doug was able to provide me with priceless insights about sex that came from his knowledge and personal experience with his patients as well as in his own marriage.

After our initial meetings Dr. Doug connected me with many staff members from his organization, Building Intimate Marriages, to help me along the process. As I sat down in meeting after meeting with different therapists, I was blown away by all they knew about sex—things I had never learned from friends, Hollywood or men's magazines. One of the points I continued to hear from the staff was that most people have sexual problems years into their marriage due to all the sexual misconceptions and baggage they bring into the relationship, which was the one thing I did not want to hear.

I want to pass on to you the valuable information I learned from these meetings. As I said previously, I am not a sex expert or a licensed therapist. But the information from the therapists at Building Intimate Marriages—what they teach people to help them have a healthy biblical framework for being a great lover in marriage—drastically changed my life (you can thank me for the info later).

Don't worry. In this chapter on being a great lover, I won't take your mind through the gutter with diagrams detailing different sexual positions. When I talk about being a great lover, I am not talking about practicing sex before marriage but about trusting in God and experiencing transformation in every area of our lives. As Dr. Gary Smalley said, "The best sex of your life starts in your heart, not in your head or between your legs."[1]

So let's begin. To get started, we're going to look at the difference between selfish sex and intimate sex.

Selfish Sex

One of the most "interesting" stories that I have read in the Bible comes in Genesis chapter 38. At the beginning of the chapter we are introduced to a man named Er who died due to his outright rebellion against God, which left his wife Tamar widowed. According to Jewish law, it was customary when a man died for his closest living male relative to marry, love, protect and care for his widow and to produce offspring for him. Therefore God commanded Onan, the brother of Er, to marry and raise a family with Tamar.

While Onan was eager to have sex with Tamar, he didn't want to marry her or provide her with children. So whenever Onan had sex with Tamar, he would, as the Bible says, "waste the semen on the ground" (Gen. 38:9), showing that he was interested in using her for a good time but not interested in giving her a good life. Instead of saying that Onan knew Tamar, which would show that he intimately cared for her, the author of Genesis wrote that Onan went into Tamar, which shows that he didn't care for her soul or well-being. He was only interested in gratifying himself with sexual pleasure.

Onan's actions are a perfect example of what Building Intimate Marriages calls selfish sex. Those who have selfish sex are concerned only with receiving personal pleasure and do not take into consideration the soul or the well-being of their partner. Selfish sex occurs whenever someone has sex outside marriage (although it can also happen within marriage). Even those who say that they are serving another person by having sex with him or her are really not serving the other person but only using and hurting that individual.

When people have selfish sex, they are subconsciously telling their partner, "I am only thankful that you are here because you satisfy my sexual needs." Their actions show that they don't care about loving their partner or keeping them faithful to God because they are using them to satisfy their own feelings.

Intimate Sex

An account of intimate sex occurs in the first sexual account in the Bible, which we see in Genesis 4:1. The verse reads that "Adam knew Eve his wife." The Hebrew word for "knew" is *yada*, which means to deeply know someone or to be known deeply by someone. What Adam and Eve experienced was not just a physical connection but an emotional and spiritual union. They fully gave themselves to one another and experienced real intimacy because of the trust, honor, commitment and security in their marriage relationship.

While selfish sex is based upon personal feelings, intimate sex is based upon God's Word. Intimate sex is not only an act of receiving; it's mainly an act of serving and pleasing the other while being served. Intimate sex is only experienced in a marriage relationship, since both persons are physically, emotionally and spiritually secure, committed, honored and intimately satisfied with one another. When people have intimate sex, they subconsciously and vocally say to their partner, "I am thankful that you are in my life so that I can love you and serve your needs." People who have intimate sex are focused on giving love and on pushing their partner toward God and not on using the other person to gratify themselves.

Secret 1: God > Sex

After learning about intimate sex, I can imagine that some of you reacted the way that I did: "I want to get married and experience intimate sex now!"

But if you are anything like me, while you have a strong desire to experience the pleasure that comes from intimate sex, you may not be ready to put in the work, effort and sacrifice necessary to experience it. You may not be fully aware of what it would cost you to sustain a healthy, intimate marriage. Studying the promises that people make to one another when they give their marriage vows helped me to understand the responsibility that comes with marriage.

"I [husband/wife] take you [wife/husband] to be my wedded [wife/husband]. [I promise] to have and to hold, from this day forward, for better, for worse, for richer, for poorer, in sickness or in health, to love and to cherish till death do us part. And hereto I pledge you my faithfulness."[2]

As you can see from this sample marriage vow, marriage is not only about receiving love. It's mainly about giving love.

I had to be honest with myself and realize that I didn't want to get married to give love; I only wanted to get married to be loved (and to have sex). I didn't want to give myself fully in service to a woman's needs; I wanted her to give herself fully in service to my own personal needs.

Am I saying that it's wrong to want to be loved and to experience a satisfying sex life in marriage? Of course not (because I know that I want to do so). The problem that you and I run into here is that we look to the wrong person to primarily satisfy our needs for love and intimacy.

If we can take time and dig deep in order to find what our hearts are longing for, we'll discover that it's not merely sex, pleasure or relationships that we long to be satisfied with—it's long-lasting intimacy with God. This is the first secret to becoming a great lover: to be completely satisfied in a deep, intimate relationship with God before trying to pursue intimate or romantic relationships with others.

Nothing in this world can completely fulfill us, because it's God, not sex, in whom our hearts desperately desire to be fully satisfied. Dr. Gary Smalley writes,

> Sooner or later we run headlong into an inescapable fact: No person on earth is capable of giving us the fulfillment we crave. We can never plug into enough people to keep our lives filled with the happiness we want. . . . By depending on people to make us happy, we not only miss the positive emotions we crave, but we also saddle ourselves with the very negative emotions we want to avoid—deep frustration, disappointment, hurt feelings, worry, fear, unrest, uncertainty and confusion. These emotions are the inevitable results of depending on a person, place or thing for fulfillment. The bottom line? We're just not wired to plug into other people as our power source.[3]

Do you find this hard to believe? If so, let me show you what I'm talking about.

I once tried an experiment in which I made a list of ten things that I wanted to get out of a sexual relationship, and I came up with the following items:

1. Pleasure
2. Happiness
3. Intimacy
4. Comfort
5. Relaxation

6. Joy

7. Love

8. Satisfaction

9. Completeness

10. Fun

Take another look at my list. Do you notice that all the things I mentioned are exactly what God offers us in a relationship with Him? See for yourself by reading the promises and declarations of God from the Psalms:

1. *Pleasure:* "You make known to me the path of life; in your presence there is fullness of joy; at your right hand are *pleasures* forevermore" (Ps. 16:11).

2. *Happiness:* "*Delight* yourself in the LORD, and he will give you the *desires of your heart*" (37:4).

3. *Intimacy:* "O LORD, you have searched me and *known* me!" (139:1).

4. *Comfort:* "You are with me; your rod and your staff, they *comfort* me" (23:4).

5. *Relaxation:* "[God] makes me lie down in green pastures. He leads me beside still waters [of *rest*]" (23:2).

6. *Joy:* "Your testimonies are my heritage forever, for they are the *joy of my heart*" (119:111).

7. *Love:* "For you, O LORD, much, are good and forgiving, abounding in *steadfast love* to all who call upon you" (86:5).

8. *Satisfaction:* "You open your hand; you *satisfy* the desire of every living thing" (145:16).

9. *Completeness:* "Whom have I in heaven but you? And there is *nothing on earth that I desire besides you*" (73:25).

10. *Fun:* "I find my *delight* in your commandments, which I *love*" (119:47).

As you can see, the sexual pleasure that we desire to experience is only a drop of water in the vast ocean of joy and satisfaction in a real, intimate relationship with God. Think about it like this: if an orgasm is the greatest natural pleasure that a person can experience on earth, how much greater is the One who created the orgasm?

Paula Rinehart, counselor and speaker, says, "Sex is God's idea, his good gift to married couples. The parameters drawn around the sexual experience are not the work of a killjoy. They are meant to enhance pleasure and freedom and lead us to our deepest longing, which is ultimately to experience union with God himself."[4]

While intimacy with another person is defined as being uncomfortably close and vulnerable with an imperfect person, intimacy with God is defined as being uncomfortably close and vulnerable with the perfect person.

God knows us so intimately that He is aware of the exact number of hairs on our heads (see Matt. 10:30). God has seen us at our best, and God has seen us at our worst, and He still promises to never leave us (see Heb. 13:5). When God looks at our physical appearance, He truly believes that we are beautiful, and He is in love with our inward and outward appearance, because He said that we are uniquely and wonderfully made (see Ps. 139:14). God is so in love with us that He was willing to pay the ultimate price and sacrifice His Son so that we could enter a relationship with Him (see John 3:16).

God is the creator of intimacy and the only One who can give us the love, commitment, honor, security, trust and affection that we so desperately desire to experience.

Secret 2: Love with No Strings Attached

What thoughts come to your mind when you think of the word "love"? Do you think of butterflies in your stomach, sweaty palms and a dangerously fast heart rate whenever you see that special someone?

If you're anything like me, when you think of love you equate it to a euphoric-like feeling. But I found out that love is not a state of being that a person is in but an action that a person does.

In reality, there is no such thing as a person being "in love." As my mentor Dhati Lewis said, "To love is to make a commitment to another person's needs and best interests at all times, regardless of the cost."[5] Loving unconditionally is the second secret to being a great lover.

Whenever most of us say that we are in love with someone, what we really mean is that we have strong affection for that individual, which is usually dependent on the physical or emotional reinforcement (good looks, funny jokes, listening ear) the person provides for us. But when that physical or emotional reinforcement goes away (or when we get tired of it), our love for that person goes away as well. Then we end up saying, "I don't know what happened between us—we just fell out of love."

When the Bible teaches about love, it talks about a sacrificial action that is given to another person withoutany strings attached:

> Love is patient and kind; love DOES not envy or boast; it is not arrogant or rude. It does not insist on its own way; it is not irritable or resentful; it does not rejoice at wrongdoing, but rejoices with the truth. Love bears all things, believes all things, hopes all things, endures all things (1 Cor. 13:4–7).

Many times we can look at the Bible's definition of love and think that it's impossible for us to emulate that kind of love—which is true. We are not able to love another person in our own strength and willpower, which is why we must first encounter love before we are able to give love. The way we encounter love is through experiencing and learning how God loves us: "In this is love, *not that we have loved God but that he loved us* and sent his Son to be the [sacrifice] for our sins" (1 John 4:10).

God's love for us has nothing to do with the things that we do for Him but everything to do with what He does for us. Even though we rebelled against God, disregarded His Word and lived our lives according to our own will, He still stepped down into human history in order to save us. To love is to serve, sacrifice for and care for others regardless of the way that the other person treats us. "We love because he first loved us" (4:19).

Secret 3: Forgiveness

If intimacy is about love, trust, security, honor and commitment in a relationship, the killer of intimacy is an unforgiving heart.

I've seen too many marriages, friendships and relationships ruined because people will not forgive one another due to past mistakes. We must all understand that we live in an imperfect world filled with imperfect people. As I always say, "There are three things that are promised in this life: death, taxes and people who will hurt us."

The essential rule for forgiveness is given by Jesus in the Gospels. One day Peter came to Jesus and asked how many times he should forgive someone if they have wronged him. He asked if it should be seventy times. Jesus responded to him by saying, "No, not seven times . . . but seventy times seven!" (Matt. 18:22, NLT).

After hearing Jesus' words, you may, as I did, grab your calculator and conclude that you can forgive someone up to 490 times, but if that person wrongs you 491 times, you are not obliged to forgive him or her anymore. Is this what Jesus was saying? Of course not.

Jesus was teaching that we should always forgive people no matter what they do, because God forgives us no matter what we do if we are in Christ. The story of the gospel is that we wrong God every day, but He continues to forgive us and love us despite all our sins from our past, present and future. We should treat other people the way we want to be treated (see Matt. 7:12); therefore, we should always forgive people when they hurt us, which is secret number three. "Be kind to one another, tenderhearted, forgiving one another, as God in Christ forgave you" (Eph. 4:32).

Secret 4: Talk the Right Talk

Sex should not be seen as taboo subject matter that we're afraid to talk about, because God made sex. I discovered from Building Intimate Marriages that even married couples often don't openly talk to one another about sex and their struggles because of the unhealthy idea that sex is a dirty topic that shouldn't be discussed in public or private. Studies have shown that one out of four men talk to no one, not even their wives, about their sexual problems or feelings.[6]

In order for us to have life-giving relationships, we have to learn how to have an open, honest and appropriate line of communication with trustworthy people in our lives about our sexual history and struggles (this should not be done with just anybody). Honesty and self-disclosure promote deep intimacy in any relationship, and it also provides much-needed healing in our lives. This is something that we can practice today with our close friends, family members and trustworthy people in our community.

Secret 5: Sex Isn't Ultimate

The last and by far the most important secret to becoming a great lover is that—as hard as this is to believe—sex isn't the key to a happy life. The worst expectation that I put on sex was believing that I would be completely satisfied in my life as soon as I experienced it. As contradictory as it sounds, you can experience sexual satisfaction without ever having sex.

When a single person experiences sexual satisfaction, it means that the individual is content in his or her own sexuality—that he or she experiences a contentment that results from knowing and valuing God's design for sexuality as the only way to experience joy and sexual satisfaction. Though this contentment isn't void of the desire to experience sexual intimacy, the person accepts that God is a good Father who has given him or her everything needed to be fully satisfied in his or her current season of life.

Not only do we as sexually satisfied singles experience contentment with our sexuality, but we also experience a peace with it: a peace with ourselves that comes from acknowledging our sexual desires and being content in our masculinity or femininity; a peace with others that comes from experiencing life-giving relationships with people of the opposite sex as well as those of the same; and a peace with God that comes from finding our ultimate fulfillment in Him and knowing that He is pleased with our lives.

These qualities of love, peace, joy, satisfaction and contentment are gifts from God that we all can experience in our singleness. Together they constitute the beauty of trusting in God's design for our sexuality.

Reflection

- What are some of the items on the list I provided that you are looking to get from sex?
- Of all the secrets to being a great lover, which one do you struggle most to live out?
- How might you have been looking for sex and marriage to solve all your problems?

7

What Men and Women Really Want from Sex

One of the most quoted romantic comedies of the modern era is the 1996 hit movie *Jerry Maguire*. In the movie Tom Cruise plays successful sports agent Jerry Maguire, who, after distributing a written mission statement to his coworkers in which he challenges the unjust business nature of their organization, loses his job, his clients and his fiancée. In an attempt to turn his life around, Jerry starts a new sports agency with the help of single mother Dorothy Boyd, a woman who became intrigued with Jerry after reading his mission statement describing his commitment to honesty and to people.

The relationship between Jerry and Dorothy is anything but ideal. Jerry is a wounded man looking for something or someone to make him whole again, and Dorothy is a single mother looking for not only a loving father to her son but also a passionate lover who can give her life new meaning. As Jerry and Dorothy's lives become more tenuous, the two grow closer together as both hope the other can make their problems go away.

Jerry eventually proposes to Dorothy, and they end up getting married. Unfortunately, however, Jerry's heart was never in the relationship, and over time his lack of affection becomes too much for Dorothy, so she suggests that they divorce so Jerry can be free to enjoy his life.

After a life-changing event that causes Jerry to rethink his life, he flies home to see Dorothy. Jerry walks into the house in the middle of a women's divorce-recovery group meeting and gives Dorothy one of the greatest speeches in romantic-movie history as he describes how meaningless his life is without her. His speech comes to its pinnacle when he says the famous line, "I love you, and *you complete me*," which finally proves to Dorothy that he loves her. The movie rightfully ends with the two living happily ever after.

After watching *Jerry Maguire* and other romantic movies, I started contemplating Jerry's philosophy, believing that there was someone out there who could complete me and make me whole. In an attempt to find that person, I spent months, even years, eagerly searching for the mythical "one" who was supposed to meet my every need and give my life meaning. Yet the problem with my search for "the one" was that this person didn't exist, because there is no special human being on this earth who can complete me and make me whole.

The most important thing I learned from my first meeting with Dr. Doug is the concept of sexual wholeness.[1] He told me that most people falsely think of marriage as the addition of two people, so they use the equation half of me plus half of him or her equals one happy, sexually satisfied relationship. But instead of seeing marriage as the addition of two incomplete people, Dr. Doug said that we should see marriage as the multiplication of two incomplete people, so that half of me multiplied by half of him or her equals one quarter of a bitter, sexually frustrated relationship. If we are longing for another person to sexually complete us, we will enter relationships looking for someone else to perfectly meet all our needs—and we will grow bitter when they don't.

Dr. Doug reiterated that we need to remember that relationships are primarily about giving, not getting; serving, not being served; pleasing, not being pleased; and loving, not being loved. He suggested that we live by a new formula—God's formula—which says that one fully sexually satisfied me multiplied by one fully sexually satisfied him or her equals one full, sexually satisfied relationship.

Dr. Doug's concept of sexual wholeness occurs when a person is fully satisfied and made whole through Jesus Christ. As we follow the Lord, we begin to experience the overwhelming unconditional love of God, which allows us to have the capacity and desire to serve and love others unconditionally.

Only when we are made sexually whole in Christ can we have healthy relationships with the opposite sex, because then we will desire to give love as much as we desire to receive love, since we've already been fully satisfied by the God who created love.

We are about to dive a little bit deeper in this chapter into the mysteries of male and female sexuality and what our hearts truly long for with sex. What we'll find out is that for most of us, sex isn't about sex.

As in the previous chapter, most of the information here was taught to me by the therapists at Building Intimate Marriages. Again, I am *not* an expert on the topic of sex; I am only a single adult like you who has been educated by some very wise people on my journey toward experiencing sexual satisfaction in my current season of singleness.

Men and Sex

While many people think that men have one-track minds that are always focused on sex (which is somewhat true), there are deeper, underlying reasons why men are so obsessed with sex. After going through meetings, readings and research, I discovered two general things that men are subconsciously looking to get from sex: *pleasure* and *affirmation* (this list is not exclusive).

Pleasure. God was the one who created pleasure, and He takes joy whenever we enjoy pleasure in its rightful context. As the psalmist wrote to the Lord, "At your right hand are pleasures forevermore" (Ps. 16:11).

Like any good gift that God created, we can either use pleasure to benefit our lives and others' or abuse it to benefit our lives at the expense of others. We men run into serious problems whenever we become "lovers of pleasure rather than lovers of God" (2 Tim. 3:4), because this causes us to abuse sex as a means of recreational pleasure as if it were some sort of sport.

Dr. Tim Gardner taught in his book *Sacred Sex* that one of the most dangerous things a man can do outside marriage is to seek the pleasures of an orgasm to fulfill his emotional needs in life. Similar to all forms of highs, as a person chases selfish, sexual pleasure simply for pleasure's sake, his or her experience will slowly diminish in value over time, which will cause the individual to need a new form of excitement or sexually deviant behavior to reach a new high (the law of diminishing returns). This endless cycle of unsatisfying pleasure leads down a slippery slope of sexual addiction and misery. I know this personally from my past addiction to pornography. Every time I went to another pornographic website, I was searching for a new high that I could never achieve, which further perpetuated my addiction.

Another thing about men and pleasure that I discovered is

that some men use sex to gain pleasure because men use pleasure to mask and escape their pain. Self-medicating with pleasure is something that I experienced during my college years. After losing my football scholarship and going through a depression, I began my sexual escapades with random girls in an attempt to make my pain go away, but the pleasure I received could not heal the pains of my heart.

As the saying goes, every man who knocks on the door of a whorehouse is looking for God. Instead of running to sexual pleasure for salvation, we as men have to learn how to depend on God for healing from our pains. Sinful pleasure comes and goes, but intimacy that comes from God and from deep relationships last a lifetime. Instead of chasing after the fleeting pleasure that comes from sin, we need to chase the true, life-giving pleasures that come from real intimacy with God and others.

Affirmation. As a young boy, I desperately desired to be affirmed by others, especially my father and mother, which is a longing I find in almost all the men I talk to. But whenever a man doesn't receive affirmation from a positive loving source, he turns to unhealthy means in order to meet his needs. One of those unhealthy means tends be either sexual attention or sexual conquest of women.

John Eldredge writes, "I have seen far too many young men commit a kind of emotional promiscuity with a young woman. He will pursue her, not to offer his strength but to drink from her beauty, to be affirmed by her and feel like a man."[2]

We men are success driven and want to be respected in every area of our lives, especially our sexual lives. I saw this especially in my life and in the lives of my teammates while playing college football. Sex was simply a competition in which each of us tried to get the most girls on our "list" in order to prove that we were a man to the others. George Gilder, in his book *Men and Marriage*, says, "For men the desire for sex is not simply a quest for pleasure. It is an indispensable test of identity."[3]

The Bible speaks of seeking the approval of men as a nasty snare that enslaves many (see Prov. 29:25). Instead of falling into the trap of using sexual pleasure to be valued and to find our identity, we have to continue to turn to Christ as the source of our value, or else we will use sex as an idol to get the affirmation and respect we desire. We have to believe that sexual competency and random sexual escapades do not give us value and worth as men—only God does.

Common misconceptions. I will never forget the day during football practice when two seniors on the team asked me where I was from. I told them that I had been born in Staten Island, New York, but raised in Atlanta, Georgia. The two started arguing, trying to figure out where I was from since I had spent significant time in both cities. So in order to clarify the situation, one of them said, "Which city was it where you got booty for the first time? That always shows where a man is from." At that time I was still a virgin, so when I told them that I had never had sex before, the guys looked at me as if I had a disease. I can still remember the shame and embarrassment I felt that day due to my lack of sexual experience.

The biggest lie that I used to believe and that many men currently believe is that in order to be a real man, a guy must be having sex with a woman (and usually more than one). Because men believe this lie, sexual promiscuity is now seen as a rite of passage and the litmus test for manhood.

In our society virginity has become the new leprosy, and men are deemed social outcasts if they do not sexually exploit women for their own self-gratification. If a man is not a real man if he is not having sex, then Jesus Christ was never a real man, because He remained a virgin His entire life.

Without having my true identity in God, I found my identity in the false teachings of manhood that our culture embraces, which taught me that sexual competence and frequency is equal to manliness. As men, we need to reject the lies of culture and embrace our identity in God as protectors of women, not abusers of women. If we don't, we will live our lives using women as sexual objects to achieve a false sense of manliness.

We men cannot use women to affirm our masculinity, because only God can affirm us as men. If we try to use women and sex to find our value, we may gain the respect of our immature "friends," but we will lose the respect of the important people in our lives, including the real men we are disregarding, the women we are abusing and the God we are shaming.

Women and Sex

Female sexuality is one of the greatest mysteries in the world—to men and to women. Since I am not a woman, I don't have any direct experience to enable me to talk about this issue. So I will rely on information I have gained from conversations with woman therapists as well as from books I have read about the issue.

In every book I have read and every meeting I have attended, I have constantly heard that female sexuality is like the female mind: complex, eloquent and not understood by most men. So in order to bring some clarity to the subject, I will speak very broadly about two things that I've discovered that women are subconsciously looking to get from sex: *romance* and *closeness*.

Romance. After I graduated from college, I worked as a preschool teacher, and I taught a class that was 90 percent female.

One thing I saw in all the little girls in my class is that each of them desired to be showered with love and romance. There is a deep desire woven into the fabric of the female to be cherished, valued, affirmed and pursued by someone—especially by the men they value.

There is nothing wrong with a woman having the God-given desire to experience romance or a deep, meaningful sexual relationship. Unfortunately, however, our society teaches women to use sex as a means to pursue love and romance, which always provides them more pain than pleasure.

Paula Rinehart, who has counseled many women, says,

> In survey after survey, women say they miss the sense of romance, of being pursued by a man just for themselves. There's a growing awareness that something beautiful between men and women is being lost in the rush to be sexual. Some call it "lost civility." The notion that a woman is a prize in her own right, worth crossing the dance floor of life to get to know deeply, is no longer assumed. Indeed, the "death of romance" we are experiencing now has become a universal moan among women.[4]

The deep emotional needs that women have for love and romance can never be fully satisfied through selfish sexual experiences. Take for example an account of the ideal female romantic experience described in the book *Secrets of Eve*:

> When we asked women to describe their ideal sexual experience, they were often about romantic setting and circumstances: candles, music, giving massages, a nice dinner out, wine or champagne, a fire in the fireplace, vacation, clean sheets, being completely alone with their partner, intimate conversation, cuddling, dancing, the beach, staying at a hotel, room service, the mountain, talking about feelings, and surprise gifts.[5]

Notice that sexual intercourse wasn't mentioned in the list of all the things these women described. This is not saying that there is something wrong with a woman who desires sex (because that is perfectly fine), but as a whole, women generally prefer nonsexual interaction for experiencing emotional gratification.

As I talked to different young women about the idea of using sex in an attempt to receive love, some objected to the idea and said, "Sex isn't anything but a means of getting pleasure. I don't want romance or anything else from it."

When I heard this, my heart broke, and I started to wonder what had happened to their feminine hearts. What had happened to the hearts of the little girls I had seen every day at my preschool that had desired to be romanced and pursued? What guy could have broken their delicate hearts? Maybe a previous boyfriend who had cheated on them? A guy they had been interested in and who had had sex with them but never talked to them again? A father who had abandoned them and their mother and left them to fend for themselves? Or was it someone close or a stranger who had sexually abused them?

Sadly, many women in today's society have experienced so many emotional wounds at the hands of men that their souls have been torn apart, leaving them numb to the emotional aspects of sex and love. This leaves them in a rut of unhealthy sexual decision making.

Women have a deep desire for intimacy, which the fleeting passion of a random hookup or casual sex will never satisfy.

Author and journalist Danielle Crittenden says, "The desire to be pursued and courted, to have sex with someone you love as opposed to just barely know, to be certain of a man's affection and loyalty—these are deep female cravings that did not vanish with the sexual revolution."[6]

The main thing I continue to tell all the women I encounter is that the key to experiencing romance is to experience romance from the author of romance Himself: God. Don't fall for the fleeting lies of cheap novels and fictional Hollywood love scenes. Instead, pursue intimacy with God and with others who love you, and don't let the false promises of ungodly, selfish sex take your heart captive. If a man has never treated you right, there is One who will never leave you, hurt you, abuse you or let you down. His name is Jesus. Trust in Him.

Closeness. The second subconscious desire that women want from sex is closeness. Paula Rinehart writes, "As women, we are designed for deep and lasting attachment—as someone's daughter, mother, aunt, sister, friend or wife. No matter what we achieve or accomplish, our lives are empty without relationships of duration and depth."[7]

Women have a deep craving for closeness. They want to be able to be vulnerable with someone and to reveal their deepest secrets to him without fear; they want someone to touch their souls and to constantly speak love, truth and grace into their lives; they want someone to look into their eyes in such a way that they know he only desires them.

Sadly, many women today grow up without loving fathers or good men in their lives, so they have never had the opportunity of experiencing this kind of healthy closeness from a man. This causes them to give their hearts and souls to anyone who promises to give them the love they are looking for. In their search for closeness, they end up desiring negative attention from men over loving attention from God, and they disregard God's gift of their unique beauty in order to live for the world's standard of being "sexy."

Women need to see that they don't need to dress provocatively and become sexually involved with men inappropriately in order to gain closeness and intimacy. By becoming fully satisfied in an intimate relationship with God, a woman has the ability to say no to men who desire to hurt them and can be satisfied and enjoy healthy relationships with others.

I will close this section with a word of encouragement, once more from Paula Rinehart: "If a [woman] has been embraced by a love as vast and powerful as the love of Jesus, [she] will know what to hope for from a man. [She] will not be willing to take the crumbs from under the table of love."[8]

Sexual misconceptions. Due to growing up with a father who had been emotionally and physically absent, Anna had always had a strong desire to feel loved and valued by a man. She felt lonely and empty, and she longed for someone who would be there to love her, affirm her and fill the void in her life. Then, as if out of divine providence, she met a guy named Javon. He was the perfect man of her dreams, and he showered her with genuine attention and intimate words of affirmation that were like sweet music to her soul.

As they grew deeper in their relationship, Javon told Anna of his desire to take their relationship to the next level by having sex. Anna, being a virgin, was hesitant to lose her virginity, because she wanted her first time to be special on her wedding day. Yet after confirming with her friends that sex was the right thing to do if she didn't want to lose Javon, she complied and gave into his demands.

After sex Javon began to act differently around Anna. What had once been life-giving, deep conversation now became soul-tearing negligence. Eventually Javon approached Anna and told her that he wanted to end the relationship because he was interested in another girl.

Crushed and devastated, as if she had just gone through a miniature divorce, Anna condemned herself. "Maybe I am not as sexually ferocious as the women in the Hollywood movies," she thought, "If I had just given into his demands more quickly, maybe he would still be with me. I guess I'm not good enough."

For the next five years, Anna went through sexual relationship after sexual relationship, hoping that one day she could give enough of herself to a man that he would eventually give her the love she desired.

Does this story sound vaguely familiar? Does it not sound like the sexual tale of so many young women in our culture?

Sadly, due to bad advice and heart-wrenching relational experiences, many women believe that being sexual with a man is the only way to keep the relationship with him. Even though this sounds terrible, the following statement is true in our culture: men will fake loving a woman to get sex, and women will fake enjoying sex with a man to get love.

My advice to women, as a loving brother, is to guard your hearts and minds to guard against the selfish men who will try to trick you by falsely promising that they'll meet your needs for intimacy, saying, "If you really loved and cared for me, you would have sex with me."

If you ever hear someone tell you that, reply, "If you really loved and cared for me, you wouldn't use me as a tool to satisfy your sexual needs. You would learn to control yourself and trust God to wait until marriage for sex, because I'm worth it." If that person continues to make sexual advances toward you, leave him, because he obviously is not the type of God-fearing man who will give you the love and intimacy that you truly desire.

Reflection

- After learning about sexual wholeness, do you believe that you have a whole sexuality? Why or why not?
- As a man, what did you learn about yourself and about women that challenges your current views of sex?
- As a woman, what did you learn about yourself and about men that challenges your current views of sex?

8

The Joy-Filled Single Life

If someone had told the nineteen-year-old me that I would become a Jesus-loving Christian, stop sleeping around, stop watching porn and stop manipulating women—and maintain that lifestyle for five years—I would have thought they were cuckoo for Cocoa Puffs. I never would have believed that all of a sudden I could go cold turkey with sex and still enjoy my life because of some Jewish carpenter who lived two thousand years ago. Yet God is alive and real; He still works miracles, changes lives and heals the hearts of men and women around the world.

As someone whose life had been oriented around sex 24/7, one of the hardest things for me after giving my life to Christ was to learn how to live without it. The first couple years of my Christian walk, I thought I was going to explode from all my sexual frustration. After learning that I could only have sex in marriage, I went from wanting to have sex with "every girl in the world" to wanting to be married to every girl in the world. I did not have any healthy relationships with women, because if I didn't see a girl as "wifey" material, as someone I could potentially have sex with in the future, I didn't want to build any type of friendship with her. It wasn't until I watched a mini-documentary from a website called Desiring God that my views of women, sex and relationships changed.

The title of the documentary was "This Momentary Marriage: The Story of Ian & Larissa";[1] it tells the remarkable story of a young couple. Larissa, who narrates the story, begins by sharing how Ian, her boyfriend at the time, got into a car accident ten months into their dating relationship. The accident was very severe, and Ian suffered a traumatic brain injury that left him severely mentally handicapped. Though Ian could barely walk, talk or even feed himself, Larissa still decided to marry Ian and love him for the rest of his life. When asked about her reasoning, Larissa simply said that though Ian couldn't do many of the secondary things of marriage, he could still lead her spiritually and love her unconditionally, which are the most important things.

After I had finished the documentary, I felt as if someone had just slapped me in the face. I knew that if I was in Larissa's shoes and someone I had been dating received a severe brain injury, I couldn't with a clear conscious say that I would still want to marry her. Even though I feel embarrassed admitting this, the truth at that time in my life was that if I wouldn't be able have sex with a woman and if her face became disfigured, I would no longer want her. Through this documentary God showed me how selfish I still was. Even though I was not having sex and hurting women physically, my heart attitudes toward women was just as wrong as someone who was doing those things.

Over time I've realized how looking at marriage only as an opportunity for sex and not having healthy relationships with women was actually fueling my sexual frustration and hindering my sexual satisfaction. While we all have a biological, physical need that sex fulfills, sex actually meets our emotional and spiritual needs for intimacy more than it does our biological ones. This is the very reason that Larissa was able to be satisfied with Ian. She understood what was most important in the relationship, which wasn't the physical aspect of being in love but the emotional and spiritual act of being loved and giving love—something we can experience in our singleness.

In the previous chapter I wrote about the different things men and women want from sex. While pointing out our differences is beneficial, even more important is learning our similarities. By recognizing the things that we have in common, I believe that we begin to more fully understand the secret to living a satisfied life during our singleness.

Different but Exactly the Same

While we as men and women are extremely different when it comes to our sexuality, there is a key framework in the way both men and women are made. Dr. John Gottman puts it like this: "The determining factor in whether wives felt satisfied with the sex, romance, and passion in their marriage is, by 70 percent, the quality of the couple's friendship. For men, the determining factor is, by 70 percent, the quality of the couple's friendship. So men and women come from the same planet after all."[2] As you can see, time and time again men and women don't simply desire sex—we both have a deep need for love and friendship, which comes from real intimacy.

As a man, I know that most men want people in their lives to encourage, support, believe in and admire them, regardless of their shortcomings. And from my conversations with different women, I've learned that women want people in their lives who value and appreciate them as a person and not just for their body.

Both of us—men and women—desperately desire respect and love, which can be found in meaningful friendship. Friendship is the greatest gift of God, and it is a healthy expression of intimacy that anyone can experience, regardless of whether they're single or married.

Friendship

Since I'm not married, my main means of sharing and experiencing intimacy—close, vulnerable friendship—comes from having relationships with people of my own gender. However, I have learned not to disregard the importance of opposite-gender relationships.

As I said previously, intimacy means being uncomfortably close and vulnerable to another imperfect person; it is cultivated by love, trust, security, commitment and honor within a relationship. While I have found it difficult to create relationships like this with people of the opposite gender, I've had to learn that it's vitally important and an outright necessity. All healthy marriages are founded upon intimate friendship, and if we don't know how to experience healthy, close friendship with people of the opposite gender now, how can we expect to do so later?

I've learned that there are two major differences between experiencing intimacy with people of the opposite gender during singleness and experiencing intimacy in marriage.

The first difference is that intimacy in marriage is being uncomfortably close and vulnerable to another imperfect person, but intimacy in singleness is being close—but not too close—and vulnerable to another imperfect person. Intimacy is not always sexual or romantic; intimacy is nonromantic as well. As I have pursued these types of relationships with the opposite sex, I've had to be very cautious to guard my heart and mind from creating unhealthy emotional connections with these individuals (see Prov. 4:23). Yet I've learned that the fear of sinning should never keep me from living out God-honoring, intimate relationships with the opposite gender.

The second difference between intimacy in marriage and intimacy in friendship is the type of love that is experienced in the relationship. The love that is present in the intimacy we experience with our friends is known as *agape* love—the mutual, selfless and passionate love between two people that does not have any sexual implications. The love present in the intimacy in marriage is agape love as well, but it also includes *eros* love—the erotic, passionate, sexual love between two people that has sexual implications.

Of the two types of love, *eros* is less necessary for a healthy relationship—and it's also the least fulfilling kind of love. While there is nothing wrong with *eros* love, as it's fun and exciting, it's not unconditional or sustaining for the long haul of a relationship. *Agape* love is what satisfies people in relationships, whether married or single. C.S. Lewis said, "Eros will have naked bodies; friendship naked personalities."[3]

An example of intimacy in friendship in the Bible is described in the relationship between David and Jonathan. When relating the nature of their friendship, the author of First Samuel says, "The soul of Jonathan was knit to the soul of David, and Jonathan loved him as his own soul" (18:1). When I first read this verse, I thought there might have been something suspect about the nature of their friendship, but this was not the case at all. This verse simply describes two friends who loved and cared about each other deeply in a completely nonromantic, nonsexual way with life-giving agape love. Enjoying this type of life-giving, healthy friendship with both men and women is

God's way of allowing us to experiencing real intimacy during our singleness.

I know that this concept may seem difficult for many to grasp, especially the part of experiencing deep friendship with people of the opposite sex, because it was for me. As I said earlier in the chapter, the first two years of my Christian walk, I did not have any female Christian friends. I was notoriously known as the jerk who didn't ever talk to girls in my community. Through much conviction of the Holy Spirit, however, I have started to see other people in my community as brothers and sisters in Christ, which has helped change the way I love, serve and enjoy others.

In order to show more practical ways of experiencing non-romantic intimacy with people of the opposite gender, let's look at some practical examples of how I have seen it work with the men and women in my church community.

Men to Women

If you are a man who wants to learn how be intimate with women in a nonromantic way, you must learn how to express your affection to women in three major ways: by forming emotional connections, giving physical affirmation and showing specific attention.

Emotional connection. You can form emotional connections with the women in your life by getting to know them on a deep emotional and nonsexual level, which will require that you listen to them talk and engage with them in meaningful, in-depth conversation while protecting their heart (see Prov. 4:23).

An example of this happened when I noticed that a girl in my community was deeply upset over something that had happened in her life. After I sat her down and had a conversation with her about her struggles (meaning that I listened to her talk for over an hour), she told me that she was so thankful for my genuine, caring heart. Because I connected with her emotionally (while guarding her heart), our friendship has grown by leaps and bounds because of that one conversation.

Physical affirmation. You can give physical affirmation to a woman by affirming her beauty in a nonsexual or perverted way and encouraging her to be confident with the body that God gave her.

This was something that I struggled with early on in my faith. I didn't like how my best friend was always giving compliments to the girls in the community. I will never forget confronting him and asking him why he told the girls that they looked beautiful. What he told me still resonates with me today: "Hey, if we don't affirm these women in their God-given beauty, other guys will do so and try to take advantage of them. We have to protect our sisters."

With all the pressure on women in today's society to look a certain way in order to receive attention from men, we as Christian men must make sure that we protect our sisters by affirming them in their God-given beauty.

Specific attention. Last, you can give specific attention to a woman and show that she is an important part of your life by doing things for her that are uniquely catered to the way she receives love.

For example, whenever I notice that a girl in my community is struggling with insecurities due to ungodly comparisons with other girls, I try to find one thing that she is really good at and affirm her in whatever it is. By giving her specific attention, I am able to help her feel more comfortable in her own skin and encourage her to become more content with the person God made her to be.

I won't lie to you and act as if I have all these things perfectly right, because I don't. But I assure you that I'm working hard to live this out every single day, even though it is extremely difficult. The most important thing that a man can do with a woman is to talk with and listen to her. If you do one thing right, do this: learn to listen to a woman's heart, and always seek to understand her before trying to be understood.

Women to Men

If you are a woman who wants to learn how to be intimate with men in a nonromantic way, you must remember that men receive love through physical connection, consistent affirmation and deep respect.

Physical connection. Unlike women, men bond through physical instead of emotional connection. Women need to engage in physical activities and hobbies with men instead of always trying to engage them in conversation.

I saw this happen when a group of women from my community went out with a group of guys to play zombie laser tag. By engaging in a physical activity with the men, the women were able to provide these guys with an outing they would remember forever. Nothing can brighten a man's day more than having a fun time out with the girls playing zombie laser tag or doing whatever else he enjoys.

Consistent affirmation. Men flourish and grow when they receive affirmation from women, so women need to affirm a man by telling him how valuable he is to the community and mentioning to him the great things that he is doing.

For example, one of my female friends affirmed me by telling me that I was a great man of God and a loving brother. When I received this gracious compliment, I began to smile like the Grinch after his heart tripled in size on Christmas. Something supernatural happens to a man when he receives affirmation from women, so, women, lift your brothers up.

Deep respect. Last, men live their lives extremely conscious of the respect that they receive. Instead of belittling and degrading men, a woman should respect and value the men in her life through her words and body language.

I'll give a negative illustration on this point. I once got into an argument with a girl in my community. For weeks after our conversation, she disrespected and belittled me through her words and negative body language. Because of the disrespect I felt from her demeanor, I didn't want to talk to her. I chose to isolate myself from her because I didn't enjoy being put down by someone in my community.

A woman must learn that men need respect desperately, and if a man doesn't feel as if he is receiving respect from a woman, he won't want to be around her. A woman who is always nagging, insulting and disrespecting a man is destroying any possible intimacy that could be cultivated in the relationship.

I know that some people may think that an overemphasis on male-female friendship could lead people to engage in illicit, unhealthy relationships. This is not true. Our opposite-gender relationships in Christ should be more than just casual friendships but examples of brothers and sisters loving each other "in all purity" (1 Tim. 5:2). Just as we should pursue deep, affectionate relationship in healthy ways with our biological siblings, so we should do the same with our brothers and sisters in Christ.

Don't Wait for Superman

One of the biggest issues I have noticed in Christian circles is that many people view being single as a disease to be cured.

Singleness becomes an obstacle to our joy and a label that we have to rid ourselves of in order to really start enjoying our lives and experiencing the intimacy we desire. Jokes such as "Ring before spring or your money back" and "Get your Mrs. degree before it's too late" at Christian colleges reflect the pressure many (especially women) feel regarding marriage.

More than anything, I don't want this book to be another "waiting for Superman" book—a long list about not doing X and Y while we wait for that perfect person to come into our life and complete us. Personally, I don't believe in the idea of waiting for the perfect person at all. And no, I'm not contradicting myself. By waiting I don't mean trusting in God and desiring to experience sex when marriage comes, which is good and healthy, but rather living our entire lives counting down the minutes until someone sweeps us off our feet so we can live happily ever after.

Even though I really want to get married, I'm not waiting for a spouse in order to experience the fullness of life; I began experiencing the fullness of life when I met Jesus. Though at times it's hard to believe, being single is a gift from God, and not being married does not make me less of a person or any less valued by God. The love and intimacy that I long for can be experienced in my season of singleness with the other men and women whom God has placed in my life.

After reading countless books and talking with many different people, I know the immense pressures that many women experience in this area of their lives. I've heard some of my women friends tell me how after seeing others get engaged time and time again, many of them having met through social media, they wonder, *What's wrong with me? Maybe I'm not lovable or desirable, or maybe God is punishing me for the sexual actions of my past.* This kind of thinking is not accurate. There is nothing wrong with you. God does love you.

As I said before, there is nothing wrong with desiring a romantic or sexual relationship or experiencing sexual desires, since God made both men and women to be sexual beings who experience sexual longing and a deep need for emotional intimacy. The desire to be in a committed, loving sacrificial relationship is a great one, but we have to accept that it's not ultimate.

If we see sex and marriage as ultimate, we will live our single lives with a woe-is-me, Eeyore-like mentality, sadly waiting for Prince Charming or Princess Cinderella to enter our lives and rescue us from our misery. Our lives will become so consumed with the wait and with what we are missing out on that we will overlook the whole point of singleness. The point is not to be obsessed with our lack of sex or our lack of a spouse; the purpose of singleness, as with any stage in life, is to experience the fullness of life—enjoying God and others.

Singleness is all about the *yes*, not the *no*. Yes, enjoy, love and know the God who crafted your soul to be satisfied in Him. Yes, enjoy your freedom by working in a career you love, starting a nonprofit for something you care about or fighting for a cause your heart breaks over. Yes, enjoy God's creation by tasting fine wine, eating great food and engaging in hobbies that you desire. Yes, enjoy meaningful, healthy relationships with those of the same and of the opposite sex, because God didn't create you to live in a box. Yes, enjoy healthy romantic relationship with somebody in whom you are interested, because there is nothing wrong with experiencing and sharing affection with others. And yes, if you find someone whom you love and want to be with for the rest of your life, marry that person. But if you don't ever get married, it's OK.

Whatever you do, don't view your single life as simply a waiting season for when you are really going to live it up. Enjoy the fullness of life today.

Reflection

- How can you intentionally love someone of the opposite sex in your community?
- Do you believe that you are waiting for Superman and viewing your singleness as a curse? How can you live life to the fullest right now?
- How can you better maximize your singleness and enjoy the fullness of life today?

Part 4

The Sexual Dilemma

9

Jesus, We (Still) Have a Problem Here

The clock showed two in the morning as my phone began to ring. I rolled out of bed, and caller ID showed that it was my best friend James. At first I was tempted to ignore his call, but for James to be calling this late at night, I knew this had to be an emergency.

When I answered the phone, James immediately confessed to having sex with one of his classmates the day before. By the disheartened tone of his voice, I could tell that he had been crying before he called.

"I can't believe that I had sex again, man," he said. "I am so sick and tired of falling into sexual sin. What's wrong with me, and why do I keep doing this to myself?"

The interesting thing about my friend James is that he is one of the most passionate Christian young men I know. He's the leader of the campus ministry at his college and on many occasions has led Bible studies on the topic of sexual purity. James is part of a weekly accountability group and is currently discipling a group of young men in his community. He reads his Bible every day and is highly involved with his local church.

Even though James has done everything right on the proverbial Christian checklist, he still managed to fall into sexual sin. No, James is not a hypocrite; he is a sinner who needs the grace of Jesus Christ to make him pure.

Purity

When most of us hear the word "purity," our minds automatically think of abstinence or virginity, but purity is far greater than those two things. A person can be a virgin and still not be pure; a person can be married and never have had an affair but still not be pure. On the other hand, a person can be pure even if he or she has had a sexually promiscuous past. Purity is not saying no to sex before marriage. Purity is not saying yes to sex in marriage. Purity is saying yes to godliness.

The Greek word for "purity" used in the New Testament is *hagneia*, which can also be translated "sinlessness of life." When we look at the word "sinlessness" and exclude ourselves from being pure because of our sexual past, we're forgetting that as Christians, our identity in Christ is based upon what Christ has done for us, not upon what we do. When God looks at us, He doesn't view us as wicked, evil, damaged goods whom He is forced to love because He couldn't find anyone better. He willingly went to the cross to die for us out of His overwhelming love for us. He views us as blameless, righteous saints.

The fact that we are blameless children of God is the reason Paul's letters to the New Testament churches always address the people as saints, not sinners. Paul even addresses the people of the Corinthian church—one of the most immoral, rebellious and sexually promiscuous churches—as saints, because their identity was founded in Christ. "To the church of God that is in Corinth, to those sanctified in Christ Jesus, called to be *saints* together with all those who in every place call upon the name of our Lord Jesus Christ, . . . grace to you" (1 Cor. 1:2-3), Paul wrote.

By holding fast to our identity as blameless saints, we understand that purity is a possibility for all of us. First John 1:9 says, "If we confess our sins, he is faithful and just to forgive us our sins and to cleanse us from all unrighteousness." As long as we submit our sexuality fully to Christ, repent, and confess to Him and to others whenever we sin, we are pure, regardless of what we have done in our past. By understanding this idea, we define purity not as our sexual actions remaining pure but as our hearts being faithful and submissive to God.

I use this definition not as a license for you to do whatever you want and exploit God's forgiveness, but to reassure God's love for you even when you fall short.

I know too many people who live their lives full of shame and self-hatred because they base their identity on the worst day of their lives. While most of us understand the importance of living faithfully for Jesus and not sinning, something that should not be taken lightly, we don't know how to continue living our lives if we do sin. That is why I don't want us to define our purity based upon a one-time event. While purity does require our own personal walk in obedience to Jesus, it is founded and rests fully upon the goodness of our God and the supernatural empowerment of His grace.

As John graciously wrote in his letter to the church, "My dear children, I am writing this to you so that you will not sin. But if anyone does sin, we have an advocate who pleads our case before the Father. He is Jesus Christ, the one who is truly righteous. He himself is the sacrifice that atones for our sins—and not only our sins but the sins of all the world" (1 John 2:1-2, NLT).

Life Battles

When some people become Christians, God drastically transforms their lives, and they don't experience the same degree of sexual struggle that they did before they were saved. I've seen this in the lives of men and women who once habitually indulged in homosexual desire but then became a Christian, married a heterosexual spouse, had children, maintained a healthy family and experienced a fully satisfied and new sexuality.

I can also attest to the firsthand effects of this supernatural transformation. After struggling with a pornography addiction for over fifteen years, God transformed my heart once I became a Christian so that I no longer desire to watch pornography, and by His grace I haven't viewed it since I came to Christ.

This kind of immediate supernatural work of God is a miraculous sign of God's grace and healing for anyone, regardless of his or her sexual history. Yet this scenario is not the case for all. Sadly, I've heard stories from many of my married friends who have struggled with pornography for years into their marriage.

The term used for God's supernatural transformation in the life of an individual is "progressive sanctification," which is the continual process of God transforming, cleansing and healing the souls of people by making them more like Jesus each day. God's work of sanctification occurs differently in each person. God transforms some people's lives in six minutes, while He may take six or even sixty years to heal others. The promise of God is, "He who began a good work in you will bring it to completion at the day of Jesus Christ" (Phil. 1:6), which means that even though complete transformation may not occur in one day, four months or even ten years, God promises to one day cleanse our souls and finish the work of healing that He started in our lives, whether in this life or in the life to come.

Don't Ever Be Ashamed

As Christians, we should never be so ashamed of our sins that we're afraid to admit our struggles to others. One of the ironic things about life is that some of the people whom we think are not struggling with sexual sin are those who struggle the most.

I experienced this during my first summer as a camp counselor.

While at camp, I had the opportunity to meet hundreds of young men from different parts of the country. In the fifth week of camp, I worked with a depressed camper named Tommy who confessed to me that he had been addicted to pornography for the past six years and hated himself because of it. Tommy was so upset with himself over his addiction that he had contemplated suicide on multiple occasions.

After sharing with Tommy about my past struggles with pornography and premarital sex, I assured him that the gospel of Jesus Christ had the power to overcome his problems. Yet Tommy still was unable to forgive himself; he still felt guilty for all the times that he had watched pornography. What was even worse about Tommy's story was his fear that his twin brother Jackson would disown him if he ever found out about the addiction.

After learning that Jackson was also at the camp, I decided to talk to him about his personal walk with God and his struggles in life. Less than ten minutes into my conversation with Jackson, I found out that he also was struggling with an addiction to pornography, and I was the first person he had ever told about his struggles.

I was shocked when I heard this. Twin brothers who lived in the same house had been struggling with the same addiction to pornography (on the same computer) for the same number of years without the other's knowledge. Stories like this should assure everyone that none of us is alone in our daily wrestles. Our brothers, sisters, friends, neighbors and coworkers struggle as well.

The biggest obstacle to sexual wholeness is silence and isolation in our sexual struggles. Studies show that 55 percent of college-age students hide their sexual behaviors from others.[1] In order to overcome our problems, we shouldn't retreat to a private island where there is no one to help; we need the helping hand of others. Being transparent with our problems is one of the most helpful ways of overcoming our struggles.

The Bible teaches that we should confess our sins and struggles instead of hiding them from others. A supernatural transformation occurs when we begin to bring our sins out in the open: "Therefore, confess your sins to one another and pray for one another, that you may be healed" (James 5:16).

I can attest to this supernatural healing, which makes a person feel as if a heavy weight has lifted off his or her chest. I experienced it when I found trustworthy people with whom I could be honest and transparent. If we're not able to be vulnerable and open to the people in our lives now, we'll not be able to be vulnerable with our spouses in the future. We must trust in the ones we love to accept us for who we are at our best of times and our worst of times.

Healthy Guilt and Unhealthy Shame

One of the most helpful things I learned about struggling with sexual sin comes from Dr. Mark Laaser, president and director of the sexual-addiction recovery ministry Faithful & True. What he passed on to me has to do with understanding the difference between healthy guilt and unhealthy shame.

When we sin, one response we can have is healthy guilt. Healthy guilt is a positive emotion that motivates us to pursue deeper intimacy with God, which will lead us to a posture of humility and a heart of repentance. A person who sins and then experiences healthy guilt says, "I did something that was bad and hurtful."

On the other hand, when we linger on our sins and short-comings, we experience unhealthy shame, a bad emotion that causes us to feel as if we're wicked people who could never be accepted by others or forgiven by God. A person who sins and experiences unhealthy shame says, "I am bad and unlovable." Unhealthy shame blocks us from experiencing the freedom and joy that come from real intimacy and a whole sexuality.

In the garden of Eden, Adam and Eve experienced un-healthy shame when they first sinned and hid from God: "And they heard the sound of the LORD God walking in the garden in the cool of the day, and the man and his wife *hid themselves* from the presence of the LORD God among the trees of the garden" (Gen. 3:8).

Instead of running toward God for healing and cleansing, Adam and Eve ran away from God due to unhealthy shame and condemnation. This is the same thing we do when we sin. We experience temporary "Christian amnesia" and forget that we serve a loving and good Father who is "gracious and merciful, slow to anger and abounding in steadfast love," that he is "good to all, and his mercy is over all that he has made" (Ps. 145:8–9).

Often I accept the truth that God has forgiven my sins but struggle with the idea of forgiving myself. This attitude shows that I think that what God did on the cross was enough for Him to forgive me but not enough for me to forgive myself, which is an offensive statement to God. It shows a heart of pride and a lack of regard for the person of Christ. We must forgive ourselves for our past mistakes, because if we don't, we only hurt ourselves and cause further damage to our sexuality.

The Supernatural Grace of God

To all who have fallen into sexual sin in the past or are currently wrestling with sexual sin, know that your identity in Christ is based upon what God has done for you and not what you do for Him.

You are not damaged goods. You are not irreparable. You have not ruined any chance of being loved and experiencing a healthy relationship in the future. While being a virgin during your singleness is a good thing and a blessing from God, not having your virginity does not make you a junior-varsity-level Christian. God still loves you, and Jesus' sacrifice for you is still sufficient.

I can easily condemn myself for my past sexual experiences and start thinking that God may withhold joy from me because of mistakes I've made in the past. Instead of trusting in the Word and the promises of God, I believe the lies of my mind, and these thoughts negatively affect my relationship with God and with others.

I have to assure myself that God isn't some tyrant sitting on a cloud in the sky ready to smite me in anger. Rather, He is a loving Father sitting on His throne, knowing that all my past, present and future sins have already been paid for on the cross by His Son Jesus Christ.

"My little children, I am writing these things to you so that you may not sin. But if anyone does sin, we have an advocate with the Father, Jesus Christ the righteous" (1 John 2:1).

We should not spend an unhealthy amount of time with our heads down, sulking about our shortcomings whenever we fall or struggle with sexual sin. Instead, we should lift up our heads and look to our Savior who loves us and died for us. It's only by God's grace that imperfect people, who fall short on a daily basis, are and will be forever blameless before a holy and perfect God. And it's through the supernatural power of the Holy Spirit that we are able to overcome our struggles.

"For by grace you have been saved through faith. And this is not your own doing; it is the gift of God, not a result of works, so that no one may boast. For we are his workmanship, created in Christ Jesus for good works, which God prepared beforehand, that we should walk in them" (Eph. 2:8–10).

Reflection

- When you sin, do you experience unhealthy or healthy guilt? How can you let go of unhealthy guilt and accept Christ's forgiveness?
- Who in your community can you ask to be your accountability partner?
- Have you come to the point at which you not only have experienced God's forgiveness but have forgiven yourself for your past? What are steps you can take to do so?

10

Did God Really Say?

The summer of 2012 was one of the most difficult seasons of my life. I went through a spiritual depression during that time, and I felt as though I were living in the valley of the shadow of death that David described in Psalm 23. The richness and joy that Bible reading and prayer had provided for me before seemed to vanish like a vapor. Time and time again I went to my knees, pleading for God to restore my joy, but it seemed as though my prayers, weighed down by my anguish and sorrow, were not breaking through the atmosphere.

One of the most difficult struggles I dealt with was sexual temptation. Since summer was in full swing, girls had traded in their fitted jeans and heavy jackets for tube tops and short shorts. Even though I knew it was wrong to lust, my heart was lured to these women as bees are drawn to the smell of sweet honey. As the depression weighed me down, what had once been innocent glances at passing women became intensive gazes, and I longed to meet the needs of my flesh.

At one of my lowest points, I was very close to acting out the selfish desires in my heart. But at the last minute the Word of God spoke to me and put everything in perspective for me: "But each person is tempted when he is lured and enticed by his own desire. Then desire when it has conceived gives birth to sin, and sin when it is fully grown brings forth death" (James 1:14–15).

Through this verse I heard God telling me that my temptation had started with my own desires, which were enticed by my feelings, emotions and thoughts on a daily basis. While there was nothing evil about my desire to experience sex, my sexual motives were based upon my needs for self-gratification during my depression. Because I lingered on my desires for an extended period of time, I had almost reached the second stage of the temptation process, which leads an individual to commit sin. If I didn't see temptation for what it truly was, I would continue to indulge these sinful desires in the hopes of experiencing a satisfaction that they could never provide, which would result in the final stage of the process: death.

The death James described wasn't a physical death in which God would strike me down with a Zeus-like thunder bolt—it was a spiritual death. This spiritual death would occur as my mind and heart became more and more numb to the will and the Word of God, which would cause me to no longer desire to obey God's will for my life, since I would be so consumed with satisfying my selfish sexual desires.

After praying diligently and meditating on that verse, I was able to see that within the bait of temptation was a hook that wanted to ruin my life. If the grace of God hadn't revealed to me the devastating consequences of willfully falling into temptation, I would have continued to be deceived by its lies and would have bitten the bait of false hope and temporary satisfaction.

The Father of Lies

As I studied more about what the Bible says about temptation, I read more about an enemy (known as Satan, or the devil) who works to tempt people and to ruin the lives of men and women on a daily basis. The Bible says that Satan was once God's most beautiful angel, but he led a foolish rebellion against God because he wanted to be worshiped as God (see Ezek. 28:12–19). God easily foiled Satan's rebellion and cast him and his followers away from His presence forever. Since he is eternally separated from God with no desire to repent, Satan's goal is to lead others with him into the damnation he will be trapped in for all eternity.

Satan first appeared in the Bible in the garden of Eden, where he tempted Adam and Eve. Though most people will say that everything that happened in Genesis 3 was Adam and Eve's fault, I would argue that if any of us had been in the same position that Adam and Eve were, we would have made the same mistake they did. Their fatal error is the same one we make each day—to believe the lies of Satan over the Word of God. Thousands of years after the Fall, we still fall for Satan's same foolish tricks, as he always begins his temptation with the phrase, "Did God really say?" (Gen. 3:1 NLT).

For example, if a man is struggling with an addiction to pornography, Satan will begin tempting him by trying to arouse this man's sexual desires. He will cause sensual women to cross the man's path, hoping that they will cause him to desire things that are forbidden by God. Though Satan knows that there is nothing wrong with a man experiencing sexual desires, he will try to make him act on his desires out of context. After Satan places women in the man's path, he begins speaking lies to this man by saying, "Did God really say that you can't watch videos or look at pictures of naked women? That can't be true. God is the One who gave you these feelings—He made you this way. What's wrong with a man beholding the beauty of God's naked creation? God isn't good to you—He's holding out on you. What could be the harm?"

Or if a young woman is struggling to keep herself pure until marriage, Satan will try to arouse desires in her heart to be sexually intimate with a guy she is interested in or with her boyfriend or fiancé. Though Satan knows that there is nothing wrong with a woman experiencing sexual desires (because women are sexual beings) or longing to love her boyfriend, he will try to make her act on her desires out of context. Once Satan does all he can to arouse her desires, he will start speaking the same lies he speaks to others: "Did God really say that you and your boyfriend can't have sex? That can't be true. God is the One who gave you both these feelings. What's wrong with two people who love each other having sex? God isn't good to you—He's holding out on you. What could be the harm?"

Satan's temptation is not only limited to those who are single, but he also tempts those who are married.

As I began to confide in others my struggles with sexual temptation, a friend of mine told me a story I will never forget about an affair he had with a coworker early in his marriage. He told me that the affair started during a period of time in which he and his wife, whom he was deeply in love with, were constantly fighting. Since there was so much animosity in their relationship, he and his wife were depriving one another of the physical, emotional and sexual intimacy they needed to sustain a healthy relationship.

In the midst of this emotionally deprived time, he noticed one of his coworkers showing him extra attention and giving him nice compliments. At first it was only innocent flirting, but this woman began providing him with the emotional affirmation that he wasn't getting from his wife. As their relationship grew closer, Satan spun his web of lies, saying, "Did God really say that you and your coworker can't have sex with one another? I mean, that can't be true. God obviously put her in your life because He knows that your wife isn't satisfying you. God isn't good to you—He's holding out on you. You are both consenting adults. What's the harm?"

After a couple weeks of Satan pestering him, my friend finally gave into the temptation by beginning a full-blown affair with his coworker. It almost destroyed his marriage, but by the grace of God his relationship with his wife was able to be restored.

Don't Believe the Lies

The Bible says that Satan is a prowling lion (see 1 Pet. 5:8) trying to "steal and kill and destroy" (John 10:10), which means that he is aggressively on the offense to destroy our lives. When Satan tempts a person, he begins by attacking the Word of God, because he wants us to question God's goodness. He wants us to believe that God's guidelines are limiting us, keeping us from true joy and satisfaction. The worst act that Satan can do is to make us believe that his ways are good and God's ways are bad.

The friend who told me about the affair with his coworker told me something else: he said that Satan always tempts us to use *inadequate* means to satisfy our *adequate* needs. Satan knows that we all have godly sexual desires that need to be satisfied. He tries to make us use the wrong means to satisfy our sexual needs by offering us temporary pleasure in place of long-lasting joy. Since he knows that we are impatient, selfish people, Satan tries to make us believe that we're missing out on something that could satisfy us.

Satan's method of getting us to use inadequate means in order to meet our adequate needs can be found in the story of Jesus' temptation in the wilderness.

In the fourth chapter of the book of Luke, we see Jesus in the wilderness fasting for forty days and forty nights. Because He fasted for such a long period of time, Jesus was hungry (see Luke 4:2), isolated and tired, which would make an ordinary man particularly susceptible to sin. Knowing that Jesus was at His lowest point physically, emotionally and spiritually, Satan seized the opportunity to tempt Jesus, hoping to catch Him off guard.

Satan began his temptation by asking Jesus to turn stones into bread in order to appease His hunger. From the outside looking in, this request seems harmless—even beneficial—to Jesus. Common sense tells us that there would be nothing wrong with Jesus using His powers to make food so that He wouldn't starve to death. Knowing that Satan is a liar, however, Jesus refused the offer and overcame the temptation by saying, "Man shall not live by bread alone, but by every word that comes from the mouth of God" (Matt. 4:4). Jesus was able to do this because He understood that Satan wasn't trying to lend Him a helping hand. Satan was trying to sabotage Jesus' life and deter Him from God's will in His life.

Prayer and Trusting in God

The Bible teaches that Jesus was tempted in every way as we are but was still without sin (see Heb. 4:15). This means that Jesus was tempted sexually in His life but was able to say no to temptation and yes to the will of God. Jesus was able to accomplish this task through the Holy Spirit, who is present in us as He was in Christ.

Similarly to his tactics with Jesus, Satan has tried to get me to use inadequate means to meet my adequate needs. For Jesus the temptation was something as innocent as bread, and for me it is sex. But through the power of the Holy Spirit, I am able to say to Satan when I'm tempted, "Man shall not live by sexual pleasure alone but by every word that comes from the mouth of God."

God has also given us the supernatural power of prayer to assist us in our battle against temptation. Prayer is nothing more than communication between man and God. During prayer we talk to God the way a child talks to his father: with love, humility and faith. When we talk to God, we should thank Him for what He has already done in our lives, and we should ask Him for His protection against temptation: "Lead us not into temptation, but deliver us from evil" (Matt. 6:13).

I know from firsthand experience that prayer is effective, because through it God has kept me from Satan's temptations. As I diligently learned to pray, the Word of God spoke to me in ways that it never had before. I was able to see that there was a door through which I could escape the temptation.

When sexual temptation comes our way (and it will for all of us), we should see it as an obstacle meant to deter us from God. We must hold fast to the promises of God's Word that His ways are the only ones that lead to true, long-lasting joy. We need to be conscious and aware of the ways in which the devil seeks to tempt us individually.

If you are currently struggling with sexual temptation as I was, do whatever it takes to flee from that sexual temptation. If you are more susceptible to sexual temptation at night, then you may have to go to sleep earlier. If you are in a dating relationship and notice that temptation is strongest when you are alone with your boyfriend or girlfriend, then you may need to avoid being alone with that person in a private setting. If a certain television show leads you to have impure thoughts, then you may need to stop watching the show.

I know that this may sound legalistic to some, but it's not. We need to take the Bible's command seriously when it says, "Let anyone who thinks that he stands take heed lest he fall" (1 Cor. 10:12). Each of us knows our struggles and weaknesses better than anyone else, so there isn't a cookie-cutter answer that applies for all our lives.

Remember, there is nothing wrong with having sexual desire or longing to experience sex in marriage, but if we focus our sexual desires on people to whom we are not married, we give Satan grounds to tempt us. We shouldn't live in fear of falling into temptation, however. Rather, we should trust that we serve a loving God who desires His children to be holy as He is Holy (see 1 Pet. 1:16). Because of His desire for us, He will do whatever it takes to keep us protected from temptation.

"God is faithful, and he will not let you be tempted beyond your ability, but with the temptation he will also provide the way of escape, that you may be able to endure it" (1 Cor. 10:13).

Reflection

- In what ways are you currently being sexually tempted?
- When you are tempted, do you feel as if the temptation is harmless or harmful? Why or why not?
- In what practical ways can you try to prevent yourself from falling into temptation?

11

The Lost Art of Saying No

In Genesis 39 we read the story of a young man named Joseph who had been sold into slavery in Egypt by the hands of his older brothers. Yet by the grace of God, Joseph had been raised to a prestigious position in Egypt as the overseer of the house of his master, Potiphar, who was the captain of the guard of Pharaoh. Not only had Joseph become a successful man with a high position in a short period of time, he was also a young, attractive man, which meant that trouble was on the horizon.

As he worked in Potiphar's house, Potiphar's wife developed an obsession with Joseph. After stalking him for a period of time, Potiphar's wife asked Joseph to have sex with her. Joseph refused her offer, but she continued to beg him for days in the hopes that he would agree. Time and time again Joseph said no.

Seeing that Joseph would not cave in to her demands, Potiphar's wife decided to do something drastic. One day when she and Joseph were the only ones in the house, she grabbed his coat and forcefully yelled, "Have sex with me!"

In order to break free of her grip, Joseph ran, his coat slipping from him as it was still in her hand, and fled from the house.

Crazy, isn't it? The first time I heard this story, I asked myself, *How was it possible that young, single Joseph was able to refuse the seduction of a beautiful older woman?* Being a single man, Joseph had to have had the same strong sexual desires I do. How was he able to accomplish such a seemingly impossible task?

When I looked at the end of the story, I realized how Joseph was able to do it: he said to Potiphar's wife, "How then can I do this great wickedness and sin against God?" (Gen. 39:9).

By understanding that his sexuality was defined by the Word of God instead of by his personal feelings, Joseph had the ability to exercise self-control over his body. He was able to say no to temptation even though his natural desires told him otherwise. Self-control was the sword that Joseph wielded in order to keep his sexual drive at bay.

Mastering Self-Control

One of the greatest tools God has provided me on my journey to experiencing true sexual satisfaction is the gift of self-control. By self-control I mean having the ability to deny fleeting desires today in order to experience greater satisfaction tomorrow. Self-control is not only the ability to control our actions, it's also being able to control our thoughts and desires. Self-control does not kill our sexual desires; rather it disciplines us to trust God and His design for sex.

One of my favorite verses in the Bible addresses the issue of self-control as it pertains to our sexuality: "This is the will of God, . . . that you abstain from sexual immorality; that each one of you know how to control his own body in holiness and honor, not in the passion of lust like the Gentiles who do not know God" (1 Thess. 4:3–5).

The Greek word for sexual immorality is *porneia*, which in layman's terms would be defined as any sexual action that is forbidden by God. As I said earlier in the book, when God designed sex for marriage, He didn't mean intercourse alone. Any action that involves genital stimulation is considered a sexual act, or sex. So if anyone does any sexual activity with someone who is not his or her spouse that is intentionally meant to arouse that person's genitals (physically or mentally), he or she is guilty of committing sexual immorality.

After reading the definition of sexual immorality, I can imagine that some of you are contemplating putting this book down because it seems as if this standard is impossible. Yet as Paul said, this is not someone's personal legalistic sexual standard—this is the will of God.

For the Bible to say that God wills for us to control our sexuality is an immense statement. The will of God caused the entire universe to come into existence. The will of God allowed us to be forgiven for all our sins through the life, death and resurrection of Jesus Christ. The will of God is the supernatural Word of God that can turn chaos into beauty, light into darkness and sinners into saints. Therefore, if God said that it was His will for us to control our bodies and to refrain from sexual immorality, it is not an unrealistic possibility for us to do so but a guaranteed promise that we can do so.

Through the supernatural power of the Holy Spirit, we are able to say no to ourselves and yes to God. I tell myself every day that I am not the person from my past who was enslaved to his feelings and emotions and to what the world teaches about sexuality. I am a child of God who is saved by Christ, which allows me to experience the gift of repentance.

The word "repentance" literally means to turn away from my sin and follow God—something equivalent to a 180-degree turn. Since God has granted us the gift of repentance, we have the power and ability to put to death our previous patterns of sin and to follow God's plan for our sexuality. Now when our desires tell us to do something contrary to the will of God, we have the ability through Christ to say no to our desires and yes to God.

Don't Lose Control

Many of my married friends tell me that self-control isn't a discipline I need to learn in my singleness only but a virtue I need to master for a lifetime. If I don't learn how to exercise self-control when I am single, they say, I will not be able to exercise self-control when I am married.

Before I became a Christian, I believed that I could live as a single man engaging in any sexual desire of my heart and then, once I got a ring on my finger, suddenly stop my promiscuity and focus on just one person. I now see how this can never happen. I have to prepare myself today to be the man I want to be in the future. There isn't a switch I can turn on when I get married that will allow me to be faithful and focused on one woman. I need to cultivate that commitment today.

During this period of singleness in which I can't have sex, I sometimes think of my denial of such experiences as a sexual fast. Similar to any type of fast, this sexual fast means denying myself certain desires of my heart for a specific season for a specific reason to bring further glory to God. Even though it is extremely difficult, I have to remember that my sexual fast is most likely not permanent, since studies show that 90 percent of people eventually get married and have sex[1] (and I hope that I will be part of that 90 percent).

By learning how to faithfully exercise self-control in my current season of sexual fasting, I am learning how to exercise self-control during any season of my life.

When I talked to one of my mentors about the concept of a sexual fast, he told me that he has gone through this kind of fast multiple times even in his marriage—during seasons of pregnancy, sickness, military service, grief due to loss and distance due to work. Yet during these seasons of sexual fast, he has still experienced sexual satisfaction and joy. That's because, as with a person who is not married, satisfaction in life comes primarily from the intimacy we receive from God and only secondly from the intimacy we receive from a spouse or from others.

I have heard it said by many people that one of the factors of a long, happy marriage is based upon the self-control that both spouses have. For example, if a married person devoted to following God's design for sexuality hasn't had sex for a period of time and sees a sexually attractive individual that he or she is not married to, that person won't give in to the desire for temporary pleasure. Rather, the married person will exercise self-control and say, "That person is attractive, but she [he] is not my spouse. I love my spouse and want to have a sexual relationship with her [him] alone."

This is the same thing I have to do as a single person. If I see someone who is sexually attractive, my first reaction shouldn't be to lust after her or enter into mental or physical sexual relationships with her. Instead, I should say, "That woman is attractive, but she is not my wife. I want to love my wife and have a sexual relationship with her alone." The process is simple. I deny myself and remain faithful to the One whom I love. Kevin Leman, author of *Sheet Music*, put it best: "The things that God asks us to do as single men and women are the very things that build up in us the character qualities we need as husbands and wives. If we short-circuit the process, we cheat ourselves, and we enter marriage inadequately prepared for a happy, long-lasting relationship."[2]

Of all the people I have talked to about self-control, not a single married couple who had engaged in premarital sex told me that they were happy that they'd had sex before marriage. Every person (both male and female) told me that they regretted their decision and that having sex before marriage had brought many negative consequences years into their marriage because they had never learned to control themselves.

I will never forget my friend's wife telling me how hurt she was that she and her husband had been sexually active before marriage. "Since he couldn't control himself by keeping me pure when we were single and everything was great, it's hard for me to trust him to be pure and to follow Jesus later on in our marriage when things become difficult," she said.

Sexual Discipline

Again, please understand that I am not saying that there is something wrong with a man or woman, whether single or married, having strong sexual desires (I know I have them). God created us as sexual beings, and there is nothing inherently evil about us wanting to experience the beauty of sexual intimacy in a Christ-centered marriage. Yet as with everything that is good in life, we need to learn how to place sex in its proper context.

Everything that has great potential for good also has great potential for harm if it is abused. Take water, for example. Water is the source of life to all of mankind. It is good and healthy, and there is nothing inherently evil about water. But water outside its proper context and without restrictions is destructive and deadly, which we can see in floods, monsoons or tsunamis.

The same argument could be made about sex. Sex is good, fun and pleasurable. There is nothing evil about sex. But sex without any proper restrictions becomes a selfish, destructive act that destroys marriages, careers, reputations and families.

Paula Rinehart said, "The sexual boundaries God establishes are a window into his heart to protect for us the goodness of all that lies inside."[3] God is aware of our physical need to experience sexual intimacy. Before there was ever a sexual revolution or an episode of BET: Uncut (basically a soft-porn television program), God knew that we would live in a super-sexualized culture. And still, before He created the universe, God designed sexual intimacy to be experienced only between a man and a woman in the context of marriage.

You see, God has created us in such a way that we can experience a deep level of intimacy with Him and with others that will allow us to be satisfied and joyful in any season. God's grace empowers us to achieve this seemingly impossible task of self-control. Most people attempt to abuse God's grace by using it as a license to sin more continuously, but we should never do that. As Paul asked, "Are we to continue in sin that grace may abound? By no means! How can we who died to sin still live in it?" (Rom. 6:1–2).

The grace of God is not only saving grace, by which God forgives us of all our sins. There is also the empowering grace of God, which gives us the freedom to live without being enslaved to sin. We don't have to pull ourselves up by our boot straps and fight the good fight alone. God's grace empowers and strengthens us to control our minds and bodies.

We must continue to apply the motto of Paul to our life. He wrote, "I can do all things through [Christ] who strengthens me" (Phil. 4:13). Paul is not saying that he has the ability through

Christ to be the greatest athlete in the world; he is saying that he can be content through any season of his life because of the love he receives through Christ. From what we see in Scripture, Paul was single and celibate throughout his ministry as an apostle. Though Paul had sexual desires just like any single man, he learned to control those desires and to experience sexual joy and satisfaction in his singleness. By finding the same peace, joy and intimacy in Christ and experiencing the love and comfort from other people that Paul did, we too can be satisfied and content throughout any season of our lives, which I know is what we all want. "For God gave us a spirit not of fear but of power and love and self-control" (2 Tim. 1:7).

I cannot lie to you and say that I haven't been tempted to sin sexually by having sex with certain emotionally fragile women whom I knew were willing. But in the midst of these situations, I've constantly reminded myself that cheap, meaningless, ungodly sex will never satisfy the true desires of my heart. I have been down this road before, and I know that it leads to a dead end filled with hurt, frustration and regret.

What keeps me motivated to stay faithful to God in my sexuality is not the fear of tarnishing my reputation, contracting an STD or being under the disciplinary wrath of God. My true and lasting motivation comes not only from a deep trust in God as a good Father but from my desire to eventually experience the truly satisfying sexual intimacy that so many married couples have told me they enjoy in a committed, Christ-centered marriage. It is a love of what is good, not a fear of what is evil, that causes me to exercise self-control and to submit my sexuality to God.

Reflection

- Do you trust in your own willpower or in the power of the Holy Spirit to help you exercise self-control?
- Do you feel as if you exercise self-control in your sexuality out of fear of consequences (pregnancy, disease, bad reputation) or out of a love for God and others?
- What practical things can you do to remind yourself daily of the importance of self-control for a lifetime?

Part 5

TRUE SEXUAL JOY AND SATISFACTION

12

Pure, Passionate Sexuality

It was a couple days before Valentine's Day, and I was sitting on a relationship panel that I had been asked to be part of at the last minute. By last minute I mean that I had literally been in bed two hours before the panel began when my friend had called and asked me to fill in because the other panelist's car had broken down.

The first question asked of us panelists was "How can a person remain single and be satisfied in his or her life?" When my turn to answer came, I was still a bit tired, since I had just gotten up, so I spoke only a brief word about sexual wholeness. I didn't want to ramble with wasted words for a long period of time, so I passed the question to the woman sitting beside me.

She introduced herself as Sam, a fifty-plus-year-old woman who was single. When I heard that she was single, I figured that she was either widowed or divorced. Then Sam revealed to us that she had never been married in her life.

My jaw hit the floor. A fifty-plus-year-old person who had never been married was like the Loch Ness Monster or Big Foot to me. I always heard stories about such people, but since I had never seen one in person, I hadn't believed that they were real.

I was so fascinated by the fact that Sam had never been married that in the middle of the discussion I leaned over and whispered to her, "So you have never been married in your entire life?" She smiled at me and replied, "Yes, I've been single all my life." I looked back at her and replied, "Wow, that is amazing."

I spent the rest of the panel session clinging to every word that Sam said, trying to soak in every ounce of wisdom that God had bestowed upon her during her years of singleness. At the end of the panel, Sam closed by telling us what had led her to decide to remain single for the rest of her life, and I remember her words as if they had been spoken yesterday.

"Many people thought there was something wrong with me because I had never been married," she said. "There was always someone trying to impose upon me what he or she felt was best for my life. But instead of listening to the words of men, I decided to receive my instruction from the voice of God. When I was in my mid-thirties and still single, I came to the decision that I wanted to follow God's will for my life, even if it meant that I would remain single for the rest of my time on earth. I heard God speak to me, and He told me that He was more than enough for me. His love was all that I needed to live a completely satisfied and fulfilled life. So I made the decision to be single, and I have never regretted that decision."

After Sam gave her breathtaking speech, I could not get her words out of my mind. *There is no way possible she was telling the truth*, I said to myself. *She can't be truly satisfied without ever marrying or having sex in her entire life.* But as I studied her face and mannerisms, I noticed a glow on her face of an individual who was truly filled with joy and with the love of Christ. The words she spoke flowed from her heart and from what she was truly experiencing. Sam had discovered the secret to experiencing true sexual joy and satisfaction.

The Journey

Since I became a Christian and started following God's design for my sexuality, my life has never been the same. I can honestly say that I am now more sexually satisfied and content in my life than I was when I was sexually active and living in sin. I receive a supernatural peace from God each day through my intimate relationship with Him as well as through meaningful relationships with others. I can truly say that everything I have written in this book is true, because I experience sexual joy and satisfaction each day.

As I have said already, I still have strong sexual desires. There are times when I believe that I could be single and perfectly content for the rest of my life, but there are also times when I "burn with passion" (1 Cor. 7:9) so badly that I want to go to Las Vegas and marry anyone (who loves Jesus and Mark Driscoll!) immediately.

The journey of experiencing true sexual joy and satisfaction is one of the most difficult journeys that I have ever gone through, but as the old saying goes, the best things in life are the most difficult things to achieve.

The Easy Way or the Hard Way

I know that some people will get to the end of this book and disagree with almost everything that I've written. They won't believe that the key to experiencing true sexual joy and satisfaction can be found only within God's design. They will say that enjoying sex only in the context of marriage is out of date and out of style. My only response to those individuals is that God is never out of date or out of style. God's design for sexuality is the best for our life, whether we choose to accept it or not.

Regardless of what I say, God has given all of us on earth the freedom to do as we please under His will, even if by doing so we hurt ourselves in the process. I've discovered that life is nothing but different multiple-choice questions with the same series of answers: either (a) God is right, or (b) self is right. So we can learn the easy way or the hard way. My hope is that God will reveal His goodness to you before you hurt yourself or the people around you as I foolishly did in my past.

The Narrow Path to Joy and Satisfaction

For those who desire to embrace God's will for their sexuality, it is important to understand that nobody is perfect. Even though I would love to believe that we all are going to live out every word in the book, the truth is that some of us are going to fall short of God's standard for our sexuality. Yet whenever we fall short, God will always provide us with supernatural aid. Through the life, death and resurrection of Jesus Christ, God has forgiven us for all our sins—those that we committed in our past, those we commit in the present and those we will commit in the future. Our journey will have many ups and downs and many hidden pitfalls. But regardless of what we go through, God promises in His Word to never leave us or forsake us (see Heb. 13:5).

I know that I have said it multiple times, but it doesn't hurt to say it again: there is no such thing as damaged goods. There is no sexual decision too gruesome for God to forgive. God's grace is not like sand in an hour glass that runs out more quickly as we make more mistakes. There is no such thing as a person who is irredeemable in the eyes of God.

As I said in the beginning, this book is not the silver bullet that will solve everyone's sexual problems. While writing it has provided me with much assistance, it cannot fully prepare me for the difficulties of my upcoming journey of following God's design for my sexuality. I think of the journey for experiencing sexual satisfaction as a war and my book as boot-camp preparation. While boot camp is of great assistance and helps a soldier prepare for battle, there isn't enough physical, mental or emotional preparation that soldiers can do to fully prepare themselves for live-action war.

When you close the pages of this book, war will begin. It happens for everyone, including me. The beauty of this journey is that we don't have to go through it alone. We have God's Word as our sword to help us overcome any difficult situation (see Heb. 4:12). We have prayer—direct access to our loving Father who happens to be the most powerful being in the universe. We also have people in our community whom we can invite to be accountability partners so that we can be honest and transparent with others about our sexuality.

God Is Enough, Really

If you don't take anything else away from this book, I hope that you'll remember the one rule for experiencing true sexual joy and satisfaction: love, trust and enjoy God.

The more I grow in my love for God, following His design for sex and my sexuality is no longer a decision that I have to consciously make but a desire that I have.

My good friend Dr. Doug Rosenau says,

> As you cultivate a more intimate relationship with God and become more intentional about conforming your heart to His, you will be more successful at creating godly sexual behaviors

and more intentional about wise choices from your renewed heart. You'll begin thinking with your heart, soul and mind rather than being led only by your hormones, emotions and selfish desires. You will become better at recognizing sinful and immature behaviors that keep you from God's best.[1]

I hope that you don't hear me saying that if a person enjoys intimacy with God and others, he or she will immediately have the best sex ever the moment he or she gets married. I've learned that as with anything I'm not accustomed to doing, creating a healthy sexual relationship in marriage will take work, sacrifice, commitment and intentionality. As Kevin Leman wrote, "Sex is one of the most amazing things God ever thought up [has intended]—but sex this good doesn't come naturally to any of us."[2]

One of the goals of trusting God's design for sex within marriage isn't to have the most euphoric, toe-curling wedding night; it's to have the most passionate, intimate life after the wedding with the one you love.

Remember, as Christians we don't wait for a spouse and for sex to start enjoying life; we live completely satisfying lives from the moment we give our lives to and trust in Jesus. While there is nothing wrong with desiring a spouse as well as sex, since they are good gifts from God, our identity and joy are founded upon the multitude of blessings that God has already lavished upon us, not on the few He has not.

As long as you remain unmarried, my hope is that you will do what I have chosen to do and embrace God's design for your sexuality in order to experience true sexual joy and satisfaction today. And if you do get married, my hope is that you will embrace God's design for your sexuality in order to experience true sexual joy and satisfaction in your marriage. Either way, the solution is always to enjoy God and others and to embrace His way as the only and best way to experience true joy and satisfaction.

"Trust in the LORD with all your heart, and do not lean on your own understanding. In all your ways acknowledge him, and he will make straight your paths" (Prov. 3:5–6).

Epilogue

I want to thank you for taking the time to read through my book. My prayer is that you were able to laugh, cry, kick, shout, smile, cringe, fuss, agree and disagree as you began taking the daunting steps with me on the journey toward true joy and satisfaction. I know that throughout the book I've talked a lot about my personal journey and my experiences with sex and sexuality, so I wanted to close our discussion by doing something a bit different.

You are about to read two letters from some older godly friends of mine whom I deeply respect. One letter is written by a married couple who have been together for over thirty-five years and the other by a single woman who has never been married. Even though these individuals' experiences with sex are exactly opposite (intimate sex versus no sex), the beauty of their stories is that these three people all experience deep levels of joy and satisfaction in their lives.

Both letters were written by individuals over fifty who are seasoned with life experience, and the words they have to impart on the subject of sex and sexuality are priceless. I hope that the wisdom they have poured out in the pages below will bless you as much as it has blessed me. Enjoy.

Bill and Kitty Murray: The Joy and Satisfaction of Real Intimacy in Marriage

Before we got married, we read that sex in marriage is a twenty-year warm-up. Man, did we laugh at that. Our motors had been running on full throttle for almost as long as we'd known each other, and we simply could not imagine sex being anything but as satisfying as it was meant to be right out of the gate. We were primed for action, and nothing could shake the vivid picture of perfection we had in our heads.

Our honeymoon, when we finally got to do what we'd been obsessed with for almost two long years, was amazing. We laid back on the hotel sheets and let out a collective breath of relief and wonder. This was what everyone had been talking about. This was it. If we'd thought about the twenty-year warm-up comment then, we would have laughed at it even harder. What did some old man who had been married that long know anyway?

But looking back, our honeymoon was a joke. It was like a first dance lesson between two awkward people with four left feet between them. Sex was hurried (naturally, why wait any longer than we had to?), and it was fumbling (because we were hurrying), and it even felt a little cheap, following as it did on the heels of sixteen months of upholstery-chewing discipline not to do it. Shame, as an instinct, doesn't go away overnight. In retrospect it wasn't all that great.

That's the key word here: retrospect. We have plenty of that commodity now, and we can tell you with the absolute certainty of personal history that sex can get better—and better—and better.

It's ironic, if you think about it. We are not young. Both of us are on the back side of fifty, which looks more like sixty with each passing day. We are fit, but there's only so much that diet and exercise can do. But honestly, none of that matters to us these days. We are having the time of our lives. It's been twenty years almost twice over since we married, and we have warmed up to a sexual temperature we did not know was possible at first.

We love daylight and variety and music. We love candles and mirrors. We love to go slow, and we love to move fast. We love writing letters to each other and burning them afterward (our kids would just die if they saw them). We love good timing and sacrificial giving. We love fulfilling each other's selfish fantasies. We love the feeling of having no shame and the sweetness of shared secrets (which is why we will not tell you our stories—the ones that would make you blush and make our kids throw up). We love each other.

The key to good sex is, of course, love. And love in marriage that starts early and endures long is the best kind. We loved each other by waiting for sex until marriage back when we were naïve about it. Love, when it comes down to it, is a decision that we make for someone else's good. Enduring love is a series of such decisions—not a perfect, unbroken strand of them but a long history of deciding to act on what is best for the person we say we love. This is why waiting for sex is such a good idea. Doing so says, "I love you enough to choose to do [or in this case, not do] something supremely difficult just for you." Hint: if you want a good marriage, you'll be saying that a lot in the years to come.

We know what a privilege it has been to enjoy a thriving sex life for over thirty-five years. We also know that this, in the end, is a gift from God rather than an outcome in an equation. But if you were to ask us, we'd tell you every single time that waiting was the right decision, one that set a foundation for a better sex life twenty years and counting down the road.

Miss Skip McDonald, One Joyful Single: The Joy and Satisfaction of Real Intimacy in Singleness

My dear fellow singles, it's been a long journey and a good one. I'm pleased that you have picked up this book to read. I wish that I'd had it when I was a young single. I'm older now, but I have learned lots along the way. I seek to please Christ with all my heart and life. Even in the midst of a great struggle early on in my single Christian life, I knew that God was for me. I just didn't know how to be for myself in the area of sexuality and singleness.

My sexual struggle started in junior high. To this day I don't remember where I got the first book—a dirty book—no pictures, just dirty words that my little eyes didn't need to read nor my imagination need to engage. I was hooked early on and sought out other dirty books I could hide and read.

This sneaky reading led to fantasies and to solo sex, known as masturbation. A hearty diet of dirty, porn images ravaged my mind and did so for many years. As I started to grow in my relationship with Christ while in college, I started longing for freedom from what had become an addiction to porn and masturbation.

I eventually began to talk about my struggles with others. Most people didn't know what to do with my struggle or my honesty. Eventually one friend seemed to really hear me; I was relieved. I felt heard, and it was helpful.

I then started on a long journey toward sexual healing and wholeness. I stopped the dirty reading long before the mind games or masturbation. How ironic it seems that even out of this kind of struggle, God called me to a lifetime of singleness. He was determined to bring me to wholeness in Him alone.

Slowly but surely my heart turned toward God and His ways. My journey became more about Him than about me. I wanted to honor Him, and in doing so I knew that I had to surrender and yield my fleshly desires to Him over and over. He showed me that my addictive, self-centered path would never lead me to fulfillment.

As I continued the roller-coaster freedom ride over the years, the mind games eventually ceased as I ingested copious amounts of Scripture. However, the masturbation was the last to die. One major step in the right direction was the realization that sexual urges weren't wrong; we were designed that way. I learned that the way I had tried to deal with them was the culprit.

Fortunately, as I learned of my identity in Christ and as His Word took root in my heart, the masturbation began to cease. I developed a walk with Jesus on a whole new level. I experienced the change agent: the Word of God through the power of the Holy Spirit. Seeing myself from God's perspective and standing on His view of me regardless of what others thought or spoke about me catapulted me toward healing and wholeness.

As I continued to pursue a love relationship with Jesus, addictive chains fell off, and freedom stepped in. Hallelujah! The longer I walked in obedience, the more I desired it. One step of obedience led to the next. God is faithful, and He provided for me every step of the way as I chose His path.

Although I am all woman, I am a free, sanctified, joyful single woman. My worth and my value originate from Christ alone. He is enough—He proves that over and over. Situations change, and people come and go; He remains. He is my constant, my solid Rock, my life giver.

May you know the love of Christ that far surpasses any love on the planet. If you do not know this love, consider studying it as a major in the classroom of life. You will be glad that you did. On Christ's love rests the foundation of my joyful existence as His beloved, single, never-married daughter.

Q & A

As I talked with my friends about my book, they asked many questions regarding their struggles to understand sexuality and the Christian life. While I could answer most of their questions on the spot due to insight I had received from the men and women at Building Intimate Marriages, I had to research issues related to some of their questions and answer them later.

I decided to compile a list of these questions and to answer them one by one. This last section addresses the "junk drawer" of random questions about sexuality that I received.

I hope that this Q & A can answer any questions about sex that you've had for a long time but have been afraid to ask or any questions that the book didn't fully cover.

1. If I can't have sex until I am married, what am I to do with my biological sexual needs now?

First, though the desire to have sex is a healthy, God-given need that generally every person experiences, it is not a biological need required for survival.

Food is a biological need for survival, as are water, oxygen and shelter—sex, on the other hand, is not. A biological need is a basic necessity of the human body for survival, which in layman's terms means that if you don't have it, you will die. Since becoming a Christian, I haven't had sex in five years, and I'm still alive, so I can assure you that a person will not die if he or she doesn't have sex.

Second, even though sex is a need that is good for our bodies, all our bodily needs have proper means of fulfillment. For example, if a person is dying of thirst, should that person drink salty sewer water in order to satisfy his or her thirst? Or if a person is hungry, should he or she pick the berries of any wild bush and eat them? Of course not. Though drinking salty sewer water and eating wild berries may temporarily satisfy a person's needs of hunger and thirst, they are not the proper substances to satisfy those needs. In reality, doing both of these actions will lead not to fulfillment but to hurt, because both of those substances are life-taking (dangerous) and not life-giving (healthy).

So in the same way that salty sewer water isn't the substance to meet our need for water, sex outside marriage isn't the substance to meet our needs of intimate sex. By having sex outside marriage, although it feels as though our sexual needs are being met, we cause harm to ourselves (and others), since we are indulging in the tainted water of sexual sin, which can never satisfy the desires of our heart.

2. I'm having sex before I am married, but I am enjoying myself. How is it possible that I cannot achieve true sexual satisfaction?

While it's true that people who are sexually active when they are single or in a nonmarital committed relationship may experience times of exciting pleasure, what they don't realize is that their sex life, and their relationship, will hit a brick wall the moment the passion goes away. Building a relationship on sex outside marriage is like building a house on sand. Things may be good for a period of time, but eventually the flood waters of hardship will come and tear down the relationship, which wasn't built on a solid foundation.

The problem with nonmarried sexual relationships is that the sex is only built on passion, excitement and blind emotions that come from the infatuation stage of the relationship—which usually occurs during the first two years. It's scientifically proven that passion and excitement from this infatuation stage will fade, and the moment the passion fades away, the sex and affection in the relationship will fade away as well. This is why most divorces happen in the early years of marriage.

As I said earlier, we must experience intimacy with God before we can share intimacy with others. Isaiah 59:2 says, "Your [sins] have made a separation between you and your God," which means that living a lifestyle of sin and disobedience separates a person from the love of God. If a person is separated from the love of God, he or she will no longer be able to experience or share love or intimacy with others. As I wrote previously, 51 percent of marriages end in divorce in our culture, which shows that sex for most people isn't blessing and nurturing the relationship. Why? It's because most people are having selfish sex based on feelings and love of self and not intimate sex based on the Word of God and love for others.

Tim Gardner says,

> Sex between a committed, Christ-focused husband and wife creates and celebrates passion and intimacy. Sex between two strangers, autoerotic sex stimulation by pornography and even sex between those who love each other but are not married—all this creates division, hurt and a sense of betrayal. It's not "just sex." It's a soul damaging experience.[1]

3. Is it a sin to kiss?

If you would have asked me before I started researching, I would have said that kissing before marriage was sinful, because kissing to me always had a sexual connotation since I had never kissed a girl (that I wasn't related to) without it leading to sex. But the more I researched the issue, I came to realize that it is possible to kiss people without attaching sexual feelings to the act.

I'm not talking about making out on the couch, which is meant to lead to an intentional genital arousal. I'm talking about a kiss on the cheek or an affectionate kiss on the lips. For example, I have kissed my mother, sister, grandmother, aunt, niece and the daughters of my friends without any sexual connotation. Also, in some cultures kissing is a sign of mutual non-sexual affection, such as we see in the Bible when it says to greet one another with a holy kiss (see 1 Thess. 5:26).

So the answer to the question about kissing goes back to the heart of the individual. There is no cookie-cutter rule that applies to everyone. It all depends on how you view kissing and what a kiss means to the person you are kissing. If both you and that person view a kiss as a sign of deep affection between two people, then there is nothing wrong with kissing. But if one or both of you view kissing in a sexual connotation, or if kissing always leads to sexual situations, I would say that it's unwise to kiss.

4. If two people love each other, why can't they start a sexual relationship?

While most people in our culture agree on the importance of sexual exclusivity, many disagree with the idea of sex being limited to marriage. They might say, "God would never limit sex to marriage. Sex is for people who care for and love one another." I remember my friend arguing with me about this, saying that marriage is only a certificate, so it doesn't matter if people are legally married as long as they are in love or married in their own eyes (or, as some would even say, in the eyes of God).

Honestly, I used to think the same way, but I did so because I didn't fully understand how marriage works. Marriage is a covenant, a promise, that a man and a woman make to one another by committing to stay with one another and love one another for the rest of their lives. This is not a secret covenant that they make in private but a public declaration made before their families, friends and community. This covenant is sealed when these individuals make this promise before God through a mediator (usually a pastor) who goes before God on their behalf. Once the covenant is finalized, the man and woman become husband and wife and one flesh in the eyes of God, the community and the state.

Two people can't be married in their own eyes, since marriage is a public, not a private, institution. If God allowed people who simply say that they love one another to have sex, then the marital structure would be pointless. Think about it: if people could marry privately on their own, then every fifteen-year-old high-school student would be married right now.

Yes, it's true that sex is a gift to be experienced between people who truly love and are committed to one another, but love isn't just a word that a person says; rather, it's an action and a commitment that two people make to each other. This commitment can only be shown and made by promising to be with one another in the lifelong covenant of marriage.

5. Is it a sin to masturbate?

Many Christians disagree when it comes to the topic of masturbation. Whether masturbation is sinful or not I honestly can't say with a clear conscience. All I know is that it's extremely difficult to masturbate without thinking about sexual thoughts, so I personally lean on the side of caution, because it's better to be safe than sinful.

When most people masturbate, they usually do so by bringing sexual images of other people to mind in order to stimulate themselves sexually. These thoughts and feelings are what the Bible calls the sin of lust. In the book of Matthew, Jesus taught His disciples the true meaning of lust when He said, "You have heard that it was said, 'You shall not commit adultery.' But I say to you that everyone who looks at a woman with lustful intent has already committed adultery with her in his heart" (5:27–28).

Jesus is saying that the sin of lust has nothing to do with the act of sexual activity but with the impure mind that desires the sexual action. Since most people masturbate as they have lustful thoughts for another individual, I see masturbation as always leading to sin because of the lustful heart and desires behind the action.

6. I know that I can't have sex in my dating relationships, but how far can I go?

I once heard someone say that anything that would be considered adultery within marriage could also be considered fornication outside marriage. What this means is that any sexual action that a married man or woman shouldn't do with someone to whom they are not married, a single man or woman also shouldn't do with someone to whom they are not married. Is this true? I'll leave that up to you to decide.

When the Bible talks about sexual sin, it never discusses it as an action. Instead it talks about sexual sin as the desire behind the action, as we previously read in Matthew 5:27–28, where we see Jesus talking about lust. So I will say it once again: any sexual action (physical or mental) that occurs outside marriage can be considered part of lust, which is considered a sin against God.

I find it hard to believe when people say that they are not intentionally trying to experience sexual feelings in making out on the couch with their girlfriend or boyfriend. While I am not trying to make absolute rules that God has not stated in His Word, I believe that we as individuals know the answer to this question about being faithful to God within our dating relationships.

Instead of trying to get as close to the fire as you can without getting burned, I advise you to stay far away from the fire so that you won't worry about being burned. The question should never be "How far is too far?" Instead, we should always ask ourselves, "How can I please God in my relationship today? How can I better love this person today and push her [or him] toward Jesus?" As I said, it is better to be safe than sinful, and you don't want to make any mistakes today that will ruin the sexual intimacy you can have with your wife or husband in the future.

7. Can you explain more in depth the difference between having selfish sexual desires and admiring someone's beauty?

There is nothing wrong with admiring the beauty of another individual. There is also nothing wrong with admiring the beauty of another individual and desiring to experience a romantic relationship with that person. God created beautiful people, and it's not evil to notice or acknowledge that these people exist. Even the authors of different books in the Bible noticed that certain individuals were beautiful in appearance (Sarah, Rebekah, Rachel, Joseph and David, for example).

Lust, as opposed to admiring beauty, happens when we start dwelling on thoughts of an individual for too long, which will cause us to desire engaging in sexual acts with that individual. I think we understand the difference in the posture of our hearts between saying that someone is beautiful and having sexual fantasies about that individual. My advice is to guard your heart. If you notice that someone is beautiful, acknowledge it—but don't dwell on thoughts of that person's beauty for long periods of time.

8. Can a person be a Christian and also have homosexual desires?

Yes, a person can be a Christian and have homosexual desires the same way that I am a Christian who has selfish heterosexual desires. What makes people un-Christlike aren't the desires they have but the actions they indulge in. There is no difference between a teenage boy who struggles with pornography and a teenage boy who struggles with homosexual relationships. Every Christian by nature has a sinful desire that rejects God's will for his or her sexuality to some degree. Whether our sexual desires are for men, women or both, we all experience sexual desires for people outside the heterosexual marriage relationship that God will provide us with.

Because we are Christians, we're saved by grace instead of our works, and we have been given the Holy Spirit to transform our lives and cleanse our souls. That transformation looks different for each individual. The transformation may take six days for some and six years for others. As with all Christians who struggle with following God's design for their sexuality, those with homosexual desires may at times struggle and fall short, but they will continue to persevere with God as new creations who continually turn away from their sins.

However, a person cannot be a Christian and continue to live a life that habitually acts upon homosexual attraction, just as a person can't be a Christian and habitually follow the desires of any other form of selfish sexuality. The Christian life is a life of repentance, and God has given us the ability to turn away from our sins.

The Bible teaches that people who habitually and unrelentingly live a sinful lifestyle show that they have never received forgiveness and were never truly saved. That includes anyone, whether those habitually engaging in homosexual desires or those pursuing selfish heterosexual desires (see Rom.1:26-27). A Christian may have lingering sexual desires against the will of God but consistently fight them and choose not to live an outright rebellious, promiscuous lifestyle. John writes, "You know that he appeared in order to take away sins, and in him there is no sin. No one who abides in him keeps on sinning; no one who keeps on sinning has either seen him or known him" (1 John 3:5–6).

9. Why am I still struggling with pornography on a consistent basis?

Bad habits are extremely difficult to break. But the key here is that they are *difficult* to break, not impossible. In the book of Matthew, Jesus spoke life-altering words that should give hope to anyone who is struggling with any type of addiction: "With man [things are] impossible, but with God all things are possible" (19:26). Even though the correct context of that verse applies to the issue of salvation, I think it also applies to our sanctification.

I used to struggle with pornography for two major reasons. The first is that I kept putting myself in environments in which I was susceptible to viewing pornography: I either stayed on the computer late at night or carelessly surfed the Internet when I was bored and alone. The second reason is that I didn't have any accountability, and I kept my struggles secret from the people around me.

In terms of the first issue, we have to realize that in our fight against sin, we either kill the sin or are killed by the sin. We need to fight against sexual sin at all costs. Whether that means putting a porn blocker on our computer or deleting the browser on our smart phones, we need to remove ourselves from the environments that are causing us to fall into sin.

As to the second issue, the Bible says in the book of James, "Confess your sins to one another and pray for one another, that you may be healed" (5:16). We must have accountability and people in our lives to whom we are comfortable talking about our struggles and shortcomings with pornography. We can't walk the walk alone as private, lone-ranger Christians. As the old saying goes, "United we stand, divided we fall." We all desperately need other Christians in our lives for accountability.

The issue with pornography is that we must dig to the root of the issue to discover the main reason we are viewing it. Many times our addiction to pornography is due to another problem we are internally wrestling with, and we're trying to use pornography as an inadequate means to meet an adequate need.

While there is a lot of good advice that I can offer to practically prevent a person from viewing pornography, I can't provide a magic formula. Many of you who are still struggling will need additional resources and professional help in overcoming your addiction (which I provide at the end of the book). A supernatural work of the Holy Spirit in redeeming the mind and heart of an individual is the only thing that will provide lasting change and true deliverance from pornography. It was only by the power of God that I was able to overcome my addiction and become transformed and renewed. So if you're really trying to overcome your struggles with pornography, spend a lot of time in prayer asking God in faith for a supernatural healing in your life.

10. If God wants us to have sex only in marriage, what am I supposed to do with my sexual drive while I am single?

This is a very difficult tension that I personally wrestle with consistently during my season of singleness. With all the hormones and sexual pressure I have, at times I feel as if I'm going to explode from sexual frustration. Through this difficult season I've had to learn to trust God to supernaturally provide for me and keep my sexual drive at bay.

One thing that we should never do is kill the sexual desires that we have during our singleness, because doing so could damage any intimacy that we could have with our future spouse. Remember sexual desires aren't sinful; they are God-given and good. It's what we do with those desires that can create a problem.

One of the biggest problems many churches have is that they overemphasize how evil and bad sex is for the single person. This causes many people to grow up thinking that sex is evil and wrong, so when they get married it can be extremely difficult for them to suddenly shift from thinking that sex is bad and nasty to realizing that sex is good and godly.

During our singleness it's best that we redirect the energy that comes from our sexual passions instead of killing it. There are many healthy ways in which we can channel our sexual drive into positive energy that can be used to serve and help other people. I redirect my energy toward serving the Lord, which includes doing community service projects, coaching football, investing in the lives of younger men or counseling my peers. I also keep myself active by doing sports or any other physical recreational activity.

I know this can be a difficult concept to understand, because it still is to me. Another thing that helps me during my singleness is trying to redirect my sexual desires to become affectionate desires and not erotic ones. Whenever I see a woman who is attractive or whenever my mind tries to take me to a sexual place with someone, I tell myself that more than having sex with that person, I want to love her. Doing this helps me to think about that person with a godly perspective, and it makes me desire to love and serve her and not use her to meet my own personal needs.

As always, prayer is the key to overcoming this battle. One prayer that I try to consistently pray is, "God, I only want to have sexual desires with my spouse one day in the future, so until then please guard my heart and my mind. Let the sexual drive that I have now be used as energy to worship, love and serve You. I know it will be a very difficult journey for me to live a pure life, but I believe that Your Holy Spirit can give me the power to accomplish it."

11. My fiancée and I will be married soon. Are you saying that it's wrong for me to have deep feelings for her before we are married?

Of course not. Never in this book did I say that there was something evil or sinful about a person loving, caring and having romantic desires for a person with whom he or she is in a nonmarital relationship. These desires are good, and they come from God. The only thing the Bible says is wrong is engaging in a sexual relationship with the person you plan to marry before you actually tie the knot.

As Christians, we should always strive to please God before we please ourselves. I believe that we please God by having deep love and showing romantic affection to the man or woman we plan to marry. But we must guard our mind and heart, because even though a woman may be a man's fiancée, she is not yet his wife. I don't want to sound pessimistic, but two of the godliest men I know were engaged to women that they didn't end up marrying. So there is no way to guarantee that a woman will be a man's wife until the moment the two of them are officially married by the church.

If you really love and care for the person you are engaged to, you'll want to protect the well-being of his or her future marital intimacy by keeping that individual pure before God. If the way in which you are currently loving, caring for and showing affection to the person you plan to marry is keeping him or her pure before God, then there is nothing wrong with the affection you have for that person.

12. If I don't practice having sex now, how will I ever know what to do in marriage? How will I know if my future spouse and I are sexually compatible?

Think about this: when Adam and Eve were created, God didn't hand them a how-to sex manual. God did not give Adam his own reality show on which he could meet Erin, Erica, Emma and Eliza in order to discover and choose a woman with whom he would be sexually compatible. God gave Adam one woman, with whom he'd never had sex, and called him to love her for the rest of his life. Why did God do this? Because in His perfect wisdom, He didn't design marriage to be about great sex with a perfect person but to be a lifetime of serving and staying with the inevitably imperfect person you've vowed to love.

I've learned from the sex therapist that sexual compatibility between two people comes neither from ecstasy (how good the sex is) nor frequency (how often they have it) but mainly from intimacy, which occurs as love, trust, security and respect deepen through the longevity of a monogamous, self-giving, covenant relationship. In reality, marriage has nothing to do with initial sexual chemistry but with the developing love and intimacy of a husband and wife over time.

Also, Adam and Eve were both virgins when they were created, and they somehow managed to put two and two together and start the entire human race. Everyone is a virgin at one point in their life, so every couple will have to go through a period in which the two are figuring each other out sexually. Contrary to what our society says, we shouldn't try to get good at sex for our spouse before we are married—we should desire to get good at sex with our spouse throughout our marriage.

As I said previously, don't think that I'm saying that the moment you get married, you'll have the best sex ever, because that's far from the truth. It will take work for sex to be good in marriage, because you and your spouse are both coming into the relationship with sexual cluelessness and baggage that will affect one another. Everyone is different, and each spouse has a different sexual road map that will take time and dedication for the other to learn. Like anything in life and marriage, a healthy sex life is a journey that will take a lot of faith in God, sacrifice, hard work and commitment.

13. Why is the Bible so intolerant of any sexuality outside marriage?

It's not that the Bible is intolerant of other forms of sexuality itself—the Bible is intolerant of sin. The word "tolerate" means to allow the practice of something that one does not necessarily like or agree with. God cannot agree with, accept or turn a blind eye to sin. God cannot allow or condone evil (see Ps. 5:4).

God's Word—not man's feelings—defines sexuality. So if God says that a form of sexuality is wrong, we should trust His words as wisdom from a loving Father and not the opinions of men. The question we should ask is, "Why is our culture so intolerant of God's view of sexuality?" The opinions of men should submit to the Word of God, not the other way around.

Everybody is intolerant of something in life. Nobody can accept everything, and if we try to stand for everything, we end up standing for nothing. If you are going to be intolerant of anything in life, be intolerant of sin. But never be intolerant of the Word or the will of God.

Notes

Chapter 1: Let's Talk about Sex

1. Brian Mustanski, "How Often Do Men and Women Think about Sex?" Psychology Today, December 6, 2011, http://www.psychologytoday.com/blog/the-sexual-continuum/201112/how-often-do-men-and-women-think-about-sex.

2. Ryan Jaslow, "Men Think about Sex Every 7 Seconds? What Study Says," CBS News, November 29, 2011, http://www.cbsnews.com/news/men-think-about-sex-every-7-seconds-what-study-says.

3. Britney Fitzgerald, "98 Percent of American Users Distrust the Information They Find on the Internet," *Huffington Post*, July 19, 2012, http://www.huffingtonpost.com/2012/07/19/american-internet-users-distrust-info_n_1686242.html.

4. Tim Alan Gardner, *Sacred Sex: A Spiritual Celebration of Oneness in Marriage* (Colorado Springs: WaterBrook, 2002), 13.

Chapter 2: Whom Do You Trust for Advice about Sex?

1. M.D. Bramlett and W.D. Mosher, "Cohabitation, Marriage, Divorce, and Remarriage in the United States" (Hyattsville, MD: National Center for Health Statistics,

2002), Vital and Health Statistic Series 23, no. 22, http://www.cdc.gov/nchs/data/series/sr_23/sr23_022.pdf.

2. Michael Leahy, *Porn University: What College Students Are Really Saying about Sex on Campus* (Chicago: Northfield, 2009), 157.

3. "Sexual Health of Adolescents and Young Adults in the United States," Henry J. Kaiser Family Foundation, March 28, 2013, http://kff.org/hivaids/report/sexually-transmitted-diseases-in-america-how-many/.

4. Chip Ingram, *Love, Sex & Lasting Relationships* (Nashville: Baker, 2004), 13.

5. William R. Mattox Jr., "Aha! Call It the Revenge of the Church Ladies," *USA Today*, February 11, 1999.

Chapter 3: A Journey to the Very Beginning

1. Stephen and Judith Schwambach, *For Lovers Only* (Eugene, OR: Harvest, 1990), 127.

2. Douglas E. Rosenau, *A Celebration of Sex: A Guide to Enjoying God's Gift of Sexual Intimacy* (Nashville: Thomas Nelson, 2002), 4.

3. Fabio Lanzoni, interview by Oprah Winfrey, *Oprah: Where Are They Now?* August 18, 2013, http://www.youtube.com/watch?v=xUF6HwUx968.

4. Dr. Ted Roberts and Diane Roberts, *Sexy Christians: The Purpose, Power, and Passion of Biblical Intimacy* (Nashville: Baker, 2010), 20–21.

Chapter 4: It's All about Me

1. Dr. Mark R. Laaser, *Healing the Wounds of Sexual Addiction* (Grand Rapids: Zondervan, 2004), 31.

2. "Internet Pornography Statistics," *Restoring Sexual Purity*, http://restoringsexualpurity.org/statistics/.

3. "Pope John Paul II on Pornography," Covenant Eyes, http://www.covenanteyes.com/2009/12/28/pope-john-paul-ii-on-pornography/

4. "Infidelity Statistics" *Statistic Brain*, http://www.statisticbrain.com/infidelity-statistics/

5. Tom Phillips, "Man Marries Pillow," *Metro*, March 9, 2010, http://metro.co.uk/2010/03/09/man-marries-pillow-154906/.

Chapter 5: Healing and a Fresh New Start

1. Laaser, *Healing the Wounds of Sexual Addiction*, 139.

Chapter 6: The Secrets to Becoming a Great Lover

1. Dr. Gary Smalley and Ted Cunningham, *The Language of Sex: Experiencing the Beauty of Sexual Intimacy in Marriage* (Ventura, CA: Regal, 2008), 16.

2. "Sample Marriage Vows, Sample Wedding Vows," Bible.org, http://bible.org/article/sample-wedding-vows.

3. Smalley and Cunningham, *The Language of Sex*, 121–22.

4. Paula Rinehart, *Sex and the Soul of a Woman: How God Restores the Beauty of Relationships from the Pain of Regret* (Grand Rapids: Zondervan, 2010), 65.

5. Dhati Lewis, "Love: A More Excellent Way," podcast audio, Blueprint Church, http://blueprintchurch.org/sermons/love-a-more-excellent-way/.

6. Laaser, *Healing the Wounds of Sexual Addiction*, 123.

Chapter 7: What Men and Women Really Want from Sex

1. Doug Rosenau and Michael Todd Wilson, *Soul Virgins: Redefining Single Sexuality* (Nashville: Baker, 2006), 97.

2. John Eldredge, *Wild at Heart: Discovering the Secret of a Man's Soul* (Nashville: Thomas Nelson, 2011), 157.

3. George Gilder, *Men and Marriage* (Gretna, LA: Pelican, 1992), 55.

4. Rinehart, *Sex and the Soul of a Woman*, 22.

5. Archibald D. Hart, Ph.D., *Secrets of Eve: Understanding the Mystery of Female Sexuality* (Nashville: Thomas Nelson, 1998), 120.

6. Danielle Crittenden, *What Our Mothers Didn't Tell Us: Why Happiness Eludes the Modern Woman* (New York: Simon & Schuster, 1999), 39.

7. Rinehart, *Sex and the Soul of a Woman*, 26.

8. Ibid., 84.

Chapter 8: The Joy-Filled Single Life

1. "This Momentary Marriage: The Story of Ian & Larissa," *Desiring God*, May 8, 2012, http://www.desiringgod.org/blog/posts/the-story-of-ian-larissa.

2. John M. Gottman, Ph.D., *The Seven Principles for Making Marriage Work: A Practical Guide from the Country's Foremost Relationship Expert* (New York: Three Rivers, 1999), 17.

3. C.S. Lewis, *The Four Loves* (New York: Harcourt Brace, 1988), 71.

Chapter 9: Jesus, We (Still) Have a Problem Here

1. Leahy, *Porn University*, 158.

Chapter 11: The Lost Art of Saying No

1. "Marriage & Divorce," American Psychological Association, http://www.apa.org/topics/divorce/index.aspx.

2. Dr. Kevin Leman, *Sheet Music: Uncovering the Secrets of Sexual Intimacy in Marriage* (Carol Stream, IL: Tyndale, 2008), 35.

3. Rinehart, *Sex and the Soul of a Woman*, 70.

Chapter 12: Pure, Passionate Sexuality

1. Rosenau and Wilson, *Soul Virgins*, 120.

2. Leman, *Sheet Music*, 13.

Q&A

1. Gardner, *Sacred Sex*, 174.

Recommended Resources

Though I completely believe in my book and how much it's going to help you in your journey to experience a fulfilled and satisfied life, I know that it's not the silver bullet for all your sexual issues. I know many of you are going to need a lot more resources and support to help you on this journey called life. Since much of what I said in the book barely touches the tip of the iceberg which is sexual wholeness, I wanted to share with you a list of a few of my favorite books and websites that helped me in my journey (in no particular order), which I know will be a blessing to you as well.

Books:

Soul Virgins by Dr. Doug Rosenau

Sex and the Soul of a Woman by Paula Rinehart

Rid of My Disgrace by Dr. Justin Holcomb

Healing the Wounds of Sexual Addiction by Dr. Mark Laaser

Pure Desire by Dr. Ted Roberts

Pure Eyes by Craig Gross

Every Young Man's Battle by Stephen Arterburn

Every Young Woman's Battle by Shannon Ethridge
    and Stephen Arterburn

Websites:

http://conquerseries.com/

http://restoringsexualpurity.org/

http://purefreedom.org/

http://xxxchurch.com/

http://www.purelifeministries.org/

https://www.faithfulandtrue.com/

http://www.covenanteyes.com/

http://biblicalcounselingcoalition.org/connect/find-a-biblical-counselor/